Parenting with Purpose

A Christian Guide to Raising Children
and Building a Christian Home

by
Yesu Vi

To You,

Thank You!

Table of Contents

Introduction:
Embracing Your Parenting Journey with Faith

Embarking on the parenting journey is akin to navigating a river that is at once tranquil and tumultuous. At the heart of this voyage lies the potential to shape souls, to mold characters, and to impart a legacy that can withstand the ebbs and flows of life's relentless currents. Within these pages, you are invited to embrace your parenting journey with a faith-filled perspective, allowing deeply rooted Christian principles to guide you in raising children who are spiritually grounded and morally robust.

Understand that this path is not traveled alone. With each step, faith is your compass and companion, providing wisdom where uncertainty resides and offering solace during trying moments. The role you play as a parent or guardian is pivotal, and the influence you wield is profound. It extends beyond the reaches of your immediate family, touching future generations and the wider community in ways that are often unseen and yet powerfully present.

Let us embark upon discovering how love and discipline intertwine, creating a sacred tapestry that honors both the heart of the child and the teachings of Christ. This integration sets the foundation for a faith-based home environment where everyone, not just the young, flourish and grow. Witness how modeling Christ-like behavior becomes the most silent yet impactful sermon your children will ever perceive, taught through the subtleties of daily life. In this setting, your actions and choices are the curriculum, and the lessons are invaluable.

As guides and guardians, we then extend this teaching to nurturing spiritual growth in our young ones. Yet remember, this is less about formal instruction and more about cultivating an environment where family devotions, scriptural engagement, and heartfelt prayers are as natural as the morning sunrise. Here, the virtues of servitude and outreach become a family mission, fostering hearts eager to give and to love beyond measure.

Communication with our children blossoms through compassion and clarity, reinforcing the importance of active listening and understanding. Within the architecture of Christian beliefs, this dialogue forms the cornerstone of providing guidance amid life's complexities. Acknowledge the moments of doubt and difficult questions that will inevitably arise, meeting them with a steadiness that is born of your conviction and the gentle grace of your faith.

Strengthening the resilient Christian family is a continuous endeavor that calls for collective worship, united prayer during challenges, and shared joy in victories. Here, you learn the delicate balance between holding fast and letting go, understanding the significance of both in the context of spiritual growth.

The family's relationship with the church community further enriches this experience. Intertwining with a broader fellowship, you discover strength in unity, access invaluable support, and contribute to church missions with shared purpose and dedication.

Equally crucial in this expedition is the integration of education and Christian values. Making discerning choices about education paths, upholding biblical truths within learning, and grappling with diverse worldviews punctuate this aspect of the journey.

The subject of discipline, when approached with purpose and love, evolves into a powerful lesson in character-building rather than a mere means to enforce order. Delve into understanding biblical disciplinary principles and nurturing long-term virtue over momentary compliance.

Worship and praise are not merely activities but the very heartbeat of a Christ-centered home. Explore the many ways to make worship an integral part of everyday life and encourage creative expression that honors God in the most authentic of ways.

As children step outside the sanctuary of home, they are greeted by the challenge of peer relationships and social complexities. Equip them with the armor of scriptural wisdom and insight, grounding them as they navigate peer pressure and prepare for the transition into their teenage years.

Mindful stewardship over our bodies and the planet reflects our reverence for God's creations. Teach your children about the interplay between their physical existence and spiritual well-being, emphasizing the significant role of health in service to God.

In a world where technology and media are omnipresent, forge a path of discernment and establish boundaries that align with Christian ethics. Shielding your children from online dangers while guiding them toward media that uplifts rather than detracts from their faith becomes a mission of vigilant love.

Your children are tomorrow's leaders, and through your guidance, their leadership can be rooted in humility and service. Encourage ethical decision-making and prepare young Christians to assume future roles in society with integrity and purposeful influence.

As you hold this book in your hands, know that you are affirming your commitment to weave a rich tapestry of faith into the very fabric of your family life. Every chapter, every page is a stepping stone to sowing a godly legacy, ensuring that your nurturing hands plant seeds that will blossom into a strong, faithful progeny. This is your invitation to embrace your parenting journey with faith, embarking on a transformative adventure with a heart full of hope and a spirit enlightened by the abiding love of Christ.

Chapter 1:
The Pillars of Christian Parenting

As we stand at the threshold of our parenting journey, armed with love and the unwavering strength of our faith, we embrace the profound responsibility of raising our children on the rock-solid pillars of Christian parenting. Woven seamlessly into the very fabric of our day-to-day lives, these pillars uphold a nurturing space where love and discipline coexist in harmonious balance, providing a steadfast foundation for our children to thrive. Our homes become havens of faith, effusing the gentle yet persistent fragrance of Christ-like behavior, where every corner reverberates with the echo of our actions more than the timbre of our words. In this sacred space, we plant the seeds of virtue and tend to them with the diligent care of a gardener tending to their garden, knowing that through our daily life, we model a blueprint of moral integrity for our little ones to emulate. Let us step forward with intention, sculpting an environment where the heart of our faith beats strongly, infusing our family's every moment with grace, wisdom, and an unwavering commitment to mirror the love of Christ in our parenting journey.

The Role of Love and Discipline

At the heart of Christian parenting lies the harmonious blend of love and discipline, each element indispensable and profoundly connected. This section delves into the transformative power of holding these two threads together, weaving a fabric strong enough to hold a child's spirit, yet delicate enough to encompass their individuality and growth.

Love, as the foremost expression of our faith, serves as the anchor in the stormy seas of parenting. It's not simply a warm feeling or an affectionate embrace, but a steadfast commitment to seek the highest good of our children. In the biblical context, love is patient, kind, and enduring. It is the wellspring of wisdom from which discipline should flow, because true discipline is rooted in love, not in anger or frustration.

Discipline, while often misconstrued as merely punitive, is essentially a form of guidance. It's the steady hand that gently corrects, the firm voice that sets boundaries, and the clear conscience that knows when leniency is the better path. As Proverbs 3:12 tells us, "For whom the Lord loves He corrects, just as a father the son in whom he delights." Thus, discipline is an act of love, a reflection of our heavenly Father's care for us.

Striking the right balance between love and discipline can be likened to gardening. Parents are called to nurture, water, and sometimes prune their young plants so that they may flourish. In times of pruning, when correction is necessary, it should be executed with precision and care, aiming to make the plant stronger and more resilient. Too much pruning, or doing so without love, might harm the plant; while too little may allow it to grow wild and directionless.

When parents set boundaries out of love, children learn to navigate the world within a safe framework. This isn't about imposing strict rules to control, but about guiding with clarity and consistency. It's essential for children to understand that boundaries are not constraints, but the solid ground on which they can stand confidently to reach for the stars.

A child's heart is tender and impressionable, calling for a parent's discipline to be seasoned with compassion. Ephesians 6:4 urges parents not to provoke their children to anger but to bring them up in the discipline and instruction of the Lord. This calls for a delicate effort to communicate expectations and consequences without breaking the spirit of the child, always keeping the door open for grace and redemption.

Love expressed through affections and affirmations gives children a sense of security and worth, which is imperative for their self-esteem. A simple 'I love you', an embrace after a fall, or a word of encouragement can fortify a child's resilience. This emotional support is the soil where confidence sprouts, enabling children to face the rigors of discipline with an understanding of their value and capabilities.

Parents must remember to discipline from a place of peace within themselves. If they act in anger or frustration, their attempt to correct may be perceived as an outburst, losing its intended purpose and possibly harming trust. Instead, parents are encouraged to take a breath, ask for wisdom in prayer, and then proceed with a gentle yet firm hand.

Discipline should also be tailored to the uniqueness of each child. What works for one might not work for another. Just as each child is fearfully and wonderfully made, so too should our disciplinary approaches honor their individuality. It's essential to understand the child's personality, temperament, and developmental stage to apply the most effective and loving form of guidance.

Furthermore, love and discipline are not solely the work of moments of correction. They are built into the daily rhythm of life. Engaging in activities together, from shared meals and family devotions to helping with homework, provides natural opportunities for parents to express love and instill discipline through example and routine.

Parents also set the stage for discipline through their own actions. If parents live a disciplined life, showing how they manage their time, fulfill their commitments, and treat others with respect, they provide a living blueprint for their children to emulate. In essence, they become the message they wish to instill.

When correction is needed, it should be elucidated why a certain behavior is not acceptable and what the expected behavior is. This dialogue allows for teaching moments rooted in love. It's not just about pointing out the wrong but guiding towards the right. Discipline here is an educational tool, illuminating the path to correct conduct.

In times when discipline seems to fail, love calls for patience. A seed may take time to germinate, and similarly, the lessons from discipline may not be immediately evident. Parents must persevere in both love and discipline, trusting that with time and consistency, their efforts will bear fruit.

Rewards and consequences are both tools of discipline, each finding its appropriate time. When children meet expectations, showing them recognition is a loving affirmation of their effort. Conversely, when they stray from what has been taught, consequences remind them of the reality that every action bears weight.

The ultimate goal of balancing love and discipline is to raise children who not only respect authority but also understand their intrinsic worth as children of God. It's about teaching them to walk in love and self-discipline, so that they may cultivate these virtues within themselves and lead lives that bear witness to the grace they have received.

In conclusion, love and discipline are the twin pillars that sustain the heart of Christian parenting. Like a tree deeply rooted and branches spreading wide, this dual foundation enables children to grow in stature and spirit. To parents who walk this journey, let love be your guide and discipline your compass, and trust in the Lord to shape the lives of your precious ones.

Establishing a Faith-Based Home Environment

Transitioning from the foundational concept of love and discipline, we turn our focus to the cornerstone of cultivating a faith-based home environment. This is where the invisible, internal values are given tangible, observable form within the walls of your home. To establish such an environment is to embrace a way of life that nods respectfully to the profound truth that every aspect of daily living can reflect the grace and teachings of Christ.

The air within a faith-based home is different; it's charged with an unmistakable serenity that comes from the Holy Spirit's presence. This is a space where worship and scripture aren't relegated to Sunday mornings but woven into the fabric of everyday life. As a parent, you become the weaver, artfully integrating faith into the mundane, so that your home becomes an echo of the love and peace found in God's embrace.

Embarking on this journey begins with intention. It means making deliberate choices to surround your family with symbols and sounds that lift the mind to the Divine. Whether it's a cross on the wall, scripture on the doorposts, or worship music filling the rooms, these are the threads that bind your home's atmosphere to the eternal.

One fundamental aspect of creating such an environment is establishing routines that foster spiritual growth. Daily prayers, before meals or bedtime, not only offer moments of gratitude but also teach children to turn their hearts to God throughout the day. As you lead by example, your little ones learn the natural rhythm of seeking guidance and giving thanks to the Creator.

In this nurturing space, conversations about faith aren't forced but flow freely and organically. Your home becomes a safe haven for questions, discussions, and even doubts. As children grow, they'll face myriad challenges and complexities. A faith-based home environment ensures they have a strong, secure foundation from which to explore and understand the world around them.

Displaying unconditional love mirrors the love of the Father and sets a powerful standard in the home. Let your children see and feel Christ's love through you, in the way you care for them, for your spouse, and for others. Love, in its purest form, doesn't just teach; it transforms, cultivating an environment where family members feel valued and understood.

Family meals are more than a time to feed the body; they're opportunities to nourish the soul. Encourage conversation about the day's happenings, interlacing discussions with parables or teachings that reflect a Christ-centered mindset. Spontaneously praying for someone who came up in conversation is another beautiful expression of bringing faith into the everyday.

Remember that your home is not merely a dwelling but a training ground for godliness and righteousness. Encouraging the practical application of scripture like sharing, forgiveness, and compassion in interactions among siblings fosters a living faith that extends beyond the individual and into the community.

Forgiveness must be paramount in your home. Regularly practice forgiveness with each other, demonstrating the freeing power that it holds, modeling after the endless grace that God offers to us. Children who witness and participate in acts of forgiveness learn to extend it to others outside the family as well.

Visual cues are instrumental. Have your children participate in creating artwork based on their favorite Bible stories or verses. Display these creations around your home as a reminder of God's word and the active role your child plays in the life of faith.

Enforcing discipline within this faith-based environment isn't about punishment; it's about guiding children back to the path of righteousness with love, patience, and scripture. When discipline is necessary, it should be consistent, explained with clarity, and always enveloped in love to maintain the nurturing nature of the home.

Community involvement is also vital as it extends the faith-based environment beyond your home and illustrates an active faith to your children. Together, participate in church activities, service projects, or missions that allow your family to live out the gospel's call to serve and love others in community contexts.

Stewardship and care for the world God has given us are crucial lessons in a faith-based home. Teach your children about the importance of looking after the environment, caring for animals, and appreciating the beauty of creation as acts of worship and expressions of gratitude towards God.

As we consider the sacred duty of establishing a faith-based home environment, it's clear that this endeavor is both a privilege and a profound responsibility. This space is where faith takes root and blossoms, where children learn the language of the Kingdom and the family stands as a beacon of Christ's love in the world. It is where the tenderness of God meets the everyday life, crafting a legacy that will ripple through generations.

With every prayer whispered, every scripture spoken, and every act of love, remember you're not just building a household; you're building a haven for hearts to grow in faith. Let every choice reflect the sacredness of this calling, creating a home where the whispers of God's love are heard in every corner, forging an unshakeable foundation for all who dwell within.

The Importance of Modeling Christ-Like Behavior

In the continued journey of nurturing your family within the embrace of faith, the significance of reflecting Christ-like behavior cannot be overstated. As Christian parents and caretakers, your personal actions speak volumes to young hearts and minds. As the saying goes, actions often speak louder than words; there is profound truth in this, particularly when it comes to instilling values in your children.

Jesus Christ serves as the perfect exemplar of living a life of love, compassion, and integrity—qualities that are quintessential to a Christian life. By emulating Christ in your daily actions, you create a living blueprint for your children to follow. This modeling inspires them not just to hear about Christian values in abstract terms, but to see them in action, woven into the fabric of daily life.

Holding yourself to the standard of Christ-like behavior does not mean striving for perfection beyond reach; rather, it's an ongoing commitment to growth and improvement. By acknowledging your flaws and seeking forgiveness when you fall short, you're teaching your children about humility and the endless grace offered by God. They learn that a Christian journey is one of constant learning and evolution, guided by divine love.

Of course, patience is a virtue that cannot be underestimated in this endeavor. Parenting presents a myriad of challenges and stressors, situations that can test the resolve of even the most dedicated. Yet, in these moments of frustration, by taking a deep breath and choosing a response that aligns with Christ's teachings, you strengthen your testimony to your children that peace is truly more powerful than anger.

Exemplifying forgiveness is just as crucial. There will be times when children make mistakes, and they will watch closely to see how you respond. By offering grace, you demonstrate the redemption and forgiveness that is central to the Gospel message. Through such real-world applications of biblical teaching, the message of Christ's sacrifice becomes tangibly relevant.

Moreover, love must be the undercurrent of all actions and teachings. Jesus emphasized the primacy of love—loving God, loving others, and loving oneself. When love directs your conversations, discipline, and decisions, you mirror the heart of God, offering your children a firm foundation on which to build their own faith.

Service and compassion, too, are hallmarks of Christ-like behavior. Whether it's helping a neighbor in need or serving within your community, by actively engaging in acts of kindness and service, you help your children understand the joy and responsibility that comes with being a follower of Christ. You are their first glimpse into the Kingdom of God—a kingdom where service to others reigns supreme.

Consistency in your Christ-like behavior also forms a thread of trust and reliability in your family. Knowing that their parent's reactions and principles are not variables but constants, children feel secure and are more likely to adopt these principles themselves. Your consistent example serves as their compass, orienting them toward the path of righteousness, even when the road is difficult and obscure.

The pursuit of truth and wisdom is another aspect of Jesus' life that must shine through in your own. Actively seek wisdom in your choices and share your journey of learning with your children. Engage with the Scriptures, not just as literature but as a living guide, demonstrating to your children how God's Word informs and shapes your everyday decisions.

While silence has its time, your vocal stances on issues of morality and faith are powerful teaching moments for your children. Stand firm in your convictions, always ready to explain why you hold fast to the tenets of your faith. In a world teeming with conflicting worldviews, your confident adherence to Christian values gives your children a clear direction and a stable platform in the midst of societal storms.

It's essential to embed joy in your life, reflecting the deep and abiding joy promised by Christ. Regardless of the circumstances, your unwavering joy will teach your children to find solace and strength in their faith, even amid life's inevitable tumults. Encouraging a spirit of joy in your household paints a picture of Christianity not as a list of obligations, but as a journey of joyous freedom.

Living out a Christ-like example also means embracing authenticity. In your moments of worship, prayer, and reflection, let your children see your deep reverence and authentic relationship with God. Avoid reducing these practices to mere routine; let them be an outpouring of your heart. This transparency will instill a respect for genuine faith and inspire your children to seek a heartfelt connection with God.

In your quest to model Christ-like behavior, remember that every small gesture can have a profound impact. The gentle way you speak to a stranger, the manner in which you deal with disappointment, the joy with which you engage in worship—these are the moments that paint a comprehensive picture of a life dedicated to Christ.

Ultimately, modeling Christ-like behavior is not a task to be checked off but a calling to be lived out. It's an invitation to you, as a parent, to continuously grow in your faith and to invite your children to embark on that same transformative journey. In doing so, you are doing more than raising morally strong children; you are nurturing future leaders, thinkers, and compassionate citizens of Heaven's kingdom on Earth.

Embrace this role with both the sobriety and splendor it deserves. Know that in every effort, God's grace is sufficient, and His strength is made perfect in weakness. So, as you model Christ-like behavior, you do not do so alone. The Holy Spirit guides you while the heavenly host cheers you on, for you are shaping generations that will carry the light of Christ into the future.

Chapter 2:
Nurturing Spiritual Growth in Children

Approaching the sacred task of nurturing spiritual growth in children demands intentionality and a deep sense of purpose. We are, in essence, gardeners of the soul, providing the light, water, and soil necessary for the tender roots of faith to take hold. This journey, embarked upon with love and perseverance, involves creating a nurturing space where scriptural truths can be sown and flourish. Recognize that every conversation, every shared moment of prayer, every act of service holds the potential to shape a child's spiritual perspective. In this holistic pursuit, patience is your ally, as spiritual growth mirrors the gradual unfolding of a bloom, each petal a lesson absorbed, a virtue embraced. Therefore, let's tenderly guide our young ones, knowing that the seeds of today's shared reflections and heartfelt devotions will blossom into a mature, unwavering faith grounded in the profound love of Christ.

Creating Purposeful Family Devotions

In the pursuit of nurturing spiritual growth in your children, family devotions stand as a pivotal practice. Tailoring these times to be purposeful and engaging will not only endow your young ones with spiritual knowledge but will also knit your family together in the shared experience of God's word. For many, the question is not why but how to create these moments that resonate and adhere to the memory and spirit of each family member.

To begin, consider the rhythm of your family life. The regularity with which you hold devotions can set the tempo for spiritual introspection and growth. Consistency is key. Whether daily or weekly, ensure these devotions become an expected and cherished part of your family routine. When a rhythm is established, hearts and minds naturally open in anticipation of the unity and learning to come.

Choose a time when all family members can be present without hurry. Perhaps it is in the quiet of the early morning, as the day unfolds, or in the evening when activities of the day are winding down. Whenever it is, guard this time as sacred, a priority that reflects its importance in your family's life.

The setting for your devotions should invite openness and comfort. Create a dedicated space, whether at the dining table or in the living room, where the family can gather without distractions. This space can be made special with a simple candle or a cross, signifying that it's time to center yourselves on spiritual matters.

Next, the content of your devotions should resonate with every member of your family. For younger children, stories filled with adventure and heroism from the Bible can capture their imagination, while teens might seek to understand how biblical principles apply to their daily lives. Balance is vital – provide a mix of scripture reading, storytelling, and practical application.

Interactive elements can transform devotion from passive listening to engaging participation. Encourage your children to ask questions, offer their thoughts, and share their feelings. Perhaps they could take turns leading the devotion, which fosters ownership and reinforces leadership qualities within a spiritual context.

Emphasize the relevance of Bible stories to modern-day issues. When children understand that the same God who was with Moses, David, or Mary is with them today, their faith can become more tangible and grounded in reality. Bridging the gap between the past and the present in this way makes the lessons learned more impactful and memorable.

Music and worship songs are a powerful element to include in your devotions. They can touch the soul in ways that words alone may not. Singing together reinforces unity and allows for emotional expression of faith. Plus, the truth carried in songs often lingers long after the devotion has ended, reinforcing the day's teachings.

Seek to personalize your devotions by incorporating your children's experiences. If one child is dealing with a challenge, find a Bible character who faced a similar situation. Show how faith provided a way through. These personalized touchpoints can make scripture deeply relevant to your children, potentially shaping their decisions and character.

Prayer should be the cornerstone of your devotions. It is a time to cast your cares upon God, to thank Him for His blessings, and to commit your family's path to His guidance. Encourage each family member to pray, fostering confidence in talking to God in their own words. This practice nurtures a personal relationship with God and an understanding that He is always accessible.

To keep children engaged, be creative in your approach. Use drama or role-playing for Bible stories, which can be both fun and illuminating. Draw out principles and themes through crafts or art, allowing children to express their faith in a way that is uniquely theirs. This not only reinforces the lesson but also caters to various learning styles.

Don't shy away from difficult subjects either. Addressing tough questions within the safe space of family devotions builds trust and provides biblical perspectives to life's complexities. These discussions can help your children to not only understand their beliefs but also to defend them when challenged by the world.

For your devotion to truly be purposeful, it must also be actionable. Conclude with a challenge for the day or week, something practical that each person can do to live out what they've learned. Whether it's showing kindness to a sibling, helping a neighbor, or standing up for what is right, these actions solidify the words and teachings of Christ in their hearts and minds.

Lastly, stay flexible and patient. There will be times when devotions may not go as planned. Sometimes, the greatest lessons are learned in these unplanned moments. Have grace for when attention spans waver or interruptions occur. The goal is not perfection in presentation, but a sincere pursuit of God's presence in your family life.

In cultivating these purposeful family devotions, you are planting seeds that will, in due time, bear fruit in the lives of your children. You are setting a foundation of faith that can withstand the challenges of life. It's an investment into their spiritual growth, one that will yield a harvest of righteousness and peace within the warm soil of a loving, faith-filled family.

Encouraging Scriptural Engagement and Prayer

In nurturing the spiritual growth of our children, engaging them in Scripture and prayer is paramount. Just as plants require consistent watering to flourish, so too do our children's spiritual lives need regular immersion in God's Word and conversations with Him. This is not merely an educational practice; it is about making the living Word a vibrant part of their everyday experience.

Begin with making the Bible accessible. Choose a children-friendly translation and create a special time each day for family scripture reading. This could be during breakfast, after dinner, or right before bedtime. The goal is not just to read the Bible but to ignite a passion for understanding God's stories and messages. Encourage questions and provide explanations, making connections to current life situations whenever possible.

Illuminating the relevance of ancient scripture in modern times can be surprisingly impactful. When your child faces challenges, guide them in finding verses that speak to their situation. Remind them of the heroes of faith who faced similar struggles and emerged with God's help. This connection between Scripture and their own lives is what transforms words on a page into a real, living guide.

Then there's prayer, a foundational pillar of a Christian life. Instill in your children that prayer isn't merely reciting words but a conversation with a loving Father who cares deeply about their joys, fears, and desires. Teach them that they can pray anywhere and anytime. By cultivating an atmosphere where prayer feels as natural as breathing, you demonstrate its power and presence.

Create a family prayer list to include everyone's requests and thanksgivings. This practice not only keeps the family updated on each other's lives but also shows the importance of bringing everything before God. As answers come, make sure to highlight and celebrate them, reinforcing the faithfulness of God in your children's minds.

Also, explore the different forms of prayer with your children. There are prayers of thanksgiving, supplication, confession, and intercession. Illuminate these through examples and encourage your children to practice these in their private prayer life, helping them to cultivate a rich and multidimensional prayer experience.

Remember to model the behavior you want to see. Your children will most likely emulate your prayer life and scriptural engagement. Do they see you turning to the Bible for guidance? Do they hear you praying fervently, with faith that your prayers are heard and answered? The example you set is powerful and persuasive.

Furthermore, don't forget the importance of memorization. Encourage your children to memorize verses, not as a task, but as a method of writing God's promises on their hearts. These verses will become anchors in times of trouble and sources of inspiration and guidance throughout their lives.

Incorporate creative methods to make scripture and prayer exciting. Use music, art, or drama to express the stories and principles in the Bible. Children remember what they actively participate in. This also helps in relating the ageless truths of scripture to their lives in a way that resonates with them.

Don't overlook the importance of silence and stillness in prayer. Educate your children about meditative prayer practices, and how spending time in quiet with God can be both calming and revelatory. Encourage them to listen for God's voice and direction and to appreciate His presence.

Prayer walks and nature engagements can also deepen a child's sense of connectedness to God. As they observe the beauty and intricacy of God's creation, they can be encouraged to communicate their awe and gratitude to Him, recognizing His handiwork in everything.

As they grow older, introduce them to more structured bible studies and encourage them to keep a prayer journal. A journal serves as a personal record of their spiritual journey, capturing their prayers, what they feel God is saying to them, and the answers to their prayers. It's a powerful keepsake that can strengthen faith over time.

Community prayer and Bible study are also important. Engage with other families, or involve your children in the church's youth groups where they can delve into the Word and pray in a larger community. This not only reinforces what you're teaching at home but also connects them with a wider support system.

Lastly, be patient and persistent. The journey of spiritual growth is a marathon, not a sprint. There will be days when it seems like your efforts are not bearing fruit. Stay the course, knowing that each seed of truth and every faithful prayer plants something eternal in the hearts of your children.

Encouraging scriptural engagement and prayer is not simply a matter of routine or tradition. It's about connecting your children to the heart of God, establishing a dialogue with the Divine that will guide them throughout their lives. As they grow in faith, they will contribute to a world that hungers for the love, wisdom, and peace that only God can provide.

Fostering a Servant's Heart Through Outreach

In nurturing our children's spiritual growth, a crucial aspect is to instill a servant's heart within them—an impulse to extend love and service beyond the four walls of home and church. Engaging in outreach provides a practical, tangible means for children to live out the compassion that Christ exemplified.

Outreach, in its essence, is venturing into the community with the aim to serve others as Jesus served the disenfranchised and the needy. For a child, the act of giving time, energy, or resources not only sows seeds of generosity but also cultivates empathy and understanding of the broader human experience.

Children watch closely, and they learn by imitating. Begin with simple acts of kindness within your neighborhood. Shoveling snow from a neighbor's driveway or delivering home-baked goods can be powerful introductions to service. The joy and satisfaction derived from these initial steps can light a spark in young hearts, drawing them toward larger acts of service.

Volunteering as a family at local shelters or food banks offers a shared experience that can strengthen familial bonds. These communal ventures allow both the joy and struggle of service to be processed together, creating a safe space for children to express their feelings and grow from them.

Moreover, consider supporting a child or family through a trusted charity. Involve your child in selecting whom to sponsor, and allow them to write letters or send drawings to them. This interaction makes the needs of others more tangible, connecting your child's heart to those in distant places.

Organizing a community clean-up day provides an opportunity for children to learn stewardship of creation. By caring for parks and natural spaces, they engage in a hands-on approach to God's command to watch over the earth. These activities teach respect for the environment and the importance of teamwork in achieving common goals.

Through mission trips, older children and teenagers can be exposed to different cultures and ways of living, which broadens their perspectives and deepens their appreciation for diversity. Planning, fundraising, and preparing for such a trip can be a transformative journey in itself, fostering leadership skills and self-reliance.

Talk to your child about the issues that matter in your community, and brainstorm ways to address them together. It's essential to guide them toward identifying needs and creating solutions, which encourages critical thinking and an active faith that looks for ways to serve.

However, ensure that these experiences aren't merely about "doing" but also about "reflecting." After each outreach activity, discuss what you have learned with your child. Ask them how the experience made them feel and what it taught them about God, themselves, and others.

Service-based learning projects, either through your church or local organizations, combine educational elements with community service, enabling children to see the real-world impact of their faith in action.

It's crucial to celebrate the small victories and the willingness to step out in service. Praise your child for their courage in trying new things, their empathy in understanding others, and their persistence when tasks are challenging.

Incorporate prayer into your outreach efforts. Before you serve, pray together for the people you will meet and for hearts open to God's leading. After serving, give thanks for the opportunity to serve and ask God for continued compassion for those in need.

While you may be tempted to shield your child from the harsher realities of life, carefully considered exposure to challenging situations can prompt significant spiritual growth. When we protect our children too much, we risk inhibiting their capacity to see and address the pain of the world through the love of Christ.

Remember, a servant's heart is attentive to the whispers of God's Spirit, which often calls us to extend grace in unexpected places. Encourage your child to be on the lookout for people and situations where they can show God's love in their everyday encounters.

Lastly, know that fostering a servant's heart is not about adding another task to your family's already full plate. It's about weaving a spirit of service into the very fabric of your lives, making outreach a natural, ongoing expression of your faith. In doing so, you model a lifestyle that reflects the values of the Kingdom, inspiring your children to carry the torch of compassionate service throughout their lives.

Chapter 3:
Communicating with Compassion and Clarity

As we delve into the heart of effective parenting, remember that true communication stretches far beyond mere words; it is a dance of patience, understanding, and love. It's about listening as much as it is about speaking, about conveying messages with a grace that echoes the voice of Christ himself. Imagine the way a gentle brook navigates the stones in its path, considerate yet unwavering - that's the model of dialogue we're aiming for with our children. Speak with a heart that's ready to embrace their world, see through their eyes, and guide with a gentle nudge. As parents, we're afforded the divine task of shaping souls, and that requires us to impart wisdom with a mix of firmness and kindness. It's in the day-to-day conversations, where we sow seeds of faith and understanding, that we prepare our children for life's complexities. Communicating with compassionate clarity isn't just about answering their questions; it's about opening doors to a conversation that honors their voice and fosters an environment where truth and love flourish.

Becoming an Active Listener to Your Child's Needs

Active listening is a cornerstone of effective communication within the family. It demonstrates to your children that their thoughts and emotions are valued, creating an environment where needs can be openly expressed and addressed. When you listen—truly listen—you're not only hearing words, but you're also seeing into the heart of your child, aligning with the scripture "My dear brothers and sisters, take note of this: Everyone should be quick to listen, slow to speak..." (James 1:19).

Listening to your child with full attention requires patience and intention. It means putting aside your immediate reactions or the day's distractions to be fully present. In this sacred space of attentiveness, your child feels safe to share their inner world, their worries, triumphs, and questions. This is the space where true understanding blossoms.

It is important to recognize that active listening involves your whole being. Your eyes can convey empathy through warm, focused attention. Your body language, through a gentle nod or a soft touch, reinforces your presence and support. By being mindful of your nonverbal cues, you create a reassuring atmosphere that invites further sharing.

When listening, it's paramount to withhold judgment. As your child speaks, they're not looking for immediate solutions or lectures. They're seeking understanding and acceptance. Let your child finish their thoughts without interruption. You might be surprised by the insight and perspective they can offer when allowed room to articulate their feelings.

Yet, active listening does not mean silent acquiescence. After your child has shared, paraphrasing their words can show that you've genuinely understood their point. This echoes the practice of Jesus who often asked clarifying questions to ensure He understood those He ministered to. "What do you want me to do for you?" (Mark 10:51) is a profound question that honors the other person's needs and desires.

Questioning, when done with sensitivity, can be a powerful tool. It allows your child to delve deeper into their thoughts and feelings. Open-ended inquiries such as "How did that make you feel?" or "What do you think might be a good solution?" encourage self-reflection and critical thinking. It empowers your child to be an active participant in problem-solving

It's essential also to recognize when to simply be a silent supporter. Sometimes your child may not seek solutions or advice, but rather the quiet affirmation of your love and God's. In these moments, shared silence can be a profound communicator of empathy and a reflection of Psalm 46:10, "Be still, and know that I am God." This stillness can be a peaceful assurance to your child's restless heart.

Active listening extends beyond the immediate conversation. It's about recalling the concerns shared in the past and following up on them. It shows your child that their words were not only heard but also remembered, and that their ongoing experiences matter to you. This thoughtful remembrance is akin to how God pays attention to the minutest details of our lives.

As the conversation comes to a close, affirm your child's courage in expressing themselves and your appreciation for the trust they've placed in you. Ending with prayer can encapsulate the moment, laying your child's concerns before God and seeking His wisdom together.

Keep in mind that active listening is a skill honed over time with practice and mindfulness. Children are keen observers and will learn the art of listening from you. Your model of attentiveness will likely inform how they interact with others.

Mistakes are inevitable in the journey of parenting. There will be times when distractions win or patience runs low, and you may fail to listen as actively as you'd like. However, the grace lies in seeking forgiveness. Apologizing to your child for these times can mend bridges and teach them about humility and the importance of seeking reconciliation, much like our relationship with our Heavenly Father.

Nurturing active listening requires cultivating the Fruits of the Spirit within ourselves—patience, kindness, goodness, and self-control.

By demonstrating these attributes, we create a home where every voice is valued, where compassionate discourse thrives, and where the love of Christ is clearly reflected in our actions and attentiveness.

Becoming an active listener to your child's needs transforms the dynamic of your relationship. It forms a bond that goes beyond the superficial, building trust and fostering an environment where your child knows they are loved, heard, and respected. This bond is the bedrock upon which their character is shaped, their faith is founded, and their spirit is nurtured.

Parents, remember that your journey in cultivating active listening is not just about hearing words—it's about understanding hearts. As you grow in this sacred practice, you'll notice how it reverberates through your child's life, echoing into their interactions with others and their relationship with God. Embrace the listening ear with all its challenges and rewards, for in doing so, you're not only strengthening your family but also echoing the love and attentiveness of our Lord.

Guidance and Correction in a Christian Context

In the walk of parenthood, moments undoubtedly arise when guidance and correction intersect with the call to foster spirituality and morality within our precious young ones. Understanding how to navigate these moments through a Christian lens is key in cultivating an environment where clarity and compassion coexist with the imperative of nurturing righteous living.

Guidance, in the Christian home, transcends mere discipline; it's about steering the tender hearts and inquisitive minds of our children towards a life that's reflective of Christ's teachings. It's about patiently illuminating the path of wisdom when the road seems fraught with the shadows of missteps and confusion.

When we consider correction, it's never merely about rectifying undesirable behavior. Instead, it's an opportunity for learning and growth, both for the child and parent. As stewards of God's little ones, we must remember that our approach to correction should mirror the grace and love that our Heavenly Father extends to us.

It's easy to let frustration guide our reactions to our children's misbehaviors. However, embracing patience as our compass ensures that our responses not only teach but also impart the understanding that while we fall short, there's always a chance for redemption. Like a shepherd gently guiding a wayward lamb back to the fold, we too must gently redirect our children when they stray.

In the practice of correction, consistency is a hallmark of love. When our children know what to expect from us, they learn to trust and feel secure within the boundaries we set. However, these boundaries are not rigid walls but rather firm handrails that guide them as they navigate life's stairs—it's about giving them the support they need without hindering their journey.

The scripture reminds us that "The Lord disciplines the one he loves," acknowledging that discipline is rooted in love. But let us also remember that this discipline is not harsh or punitive; it's corrective and nurturing. It's important to clarify the 'why' behind our discipline to our children. This clarity fosters understanding and helps our children learn discernment.

Forgiveness is a powerful tool in the Christian parent's arsenal. Not just in offering it, but in teaching its value. When children make mistakes, it's a pivotal moment to guide them in seeking forgiveness, as well as understanding the weight and liberation that genuine repentance brings.

In moments when we must guide our children away from wrong, let's lead the conversation with love rather than lead with the wrong itself. Start by affirming the child's inherent worth and goodness, then explain how their actions are not in alignment with who they are and who they are called to be.

Prayer is essential in moments of guidance and correction. It invites the wisdom and peace of the Holy Spirit into challenging circumstances. When we pause to pray with our children, we teach them to seek God's guidance above all and demonstrate that we too are under His authority and seeking His wisdom in our parenting.

It is also vital to celebrate the moments when our children display growth and understanding. Positive reinforcement fortifies their desire to choose right over wrong. The joy in their eyes when they feel proud of their actions is a reflection of the joy in the Lord when we walk in His ways.

Be an example of the grace and humility we wish to instill. Our children watch us more closely than we sometimes realize. Admitting when we are wrong and asking for their forgiveness sets a powerful precedent for humility and sets the stage for mutual respect within the family.

Utilize stories from scripture to illustrate points of guidance and correction. Biblical narratives provide rich soil for discussions about character, choices, and consequences, and help children see these truths played out in memorable and meaningful ways.

Empathy is an essential thread woven through the fabric of compassionate correction. Let's try to understand and empathize with the struggle behind the action. This doesn't mean excusing wrong behavior, but it does mean addressing it with an understanding heart.

Remember that correction should always be age-appropriate, and should never compromise a child's dignity. As our children grow, their understanding and responsibilities will evolve, and so should our methods of guidance and correction. It's about ensuring that the manner in which we correct aligns with their level of comprehension and their developmental stage.

Indeed, guidance and correction within a Christian context is not just about raising well-behaved children; it's about raising children who embody the fruits of the Spirit. Through compassionate communication rooted in Christian love, we are helping shape their hearts and minds to reflect God's glory in every thread of their character.

Handling Difficult Questions and Doubts

A crucial component of nurturing a spiritually grounded family is learning to communicate with compassion and clarity, especially when faced with the inevitable difficult questions and doubts that arise in the minds of our children. As parents rooted in faith, we must prepare ourselves to guide our children through the complexities of life with wisdom and understanding.

When children approach us with hard questions about God, faith, or moral dilemmas, first and foremost, it's essential to listen with an open heart. Engaging in an active listening mode does more than hear the words; it demonstrates respect for their curiosity and a genuine interest in their personal growth. Remember, the way we respond can either strengthen their trust in the Lord or push them away.

It's important to acknowledge that not all questions have immediate answers. Admitting that you need time to think or that you're unsure can be an act of humility that teaches your child the value of seeking wisdom. Use these moments to foster a partnership in finding answers, perhaps by researching the Bible together or bringing the question to a pastor or trusted Christian friend.

Acknowledge the validity of their doubts without judgment. Even the disciples had moments of uncertainty, and it's a natural part of faith development. Lead the conversation with empathy, sharing that you, too, have had questions and have sometimes struggled to reconcile difficult truths.

Instill in your children the confidence that God's character is unchanging. Remind them that even when we do not understand, we can trust in His nature—His goodness, love, and justice—and rest in the knowledge that His ways are higher than ours. Encourage them to see doubts not as a weakness in faith but as a step towards a deeper understanding.

Children are incredibly perceptive and will often mirror our attitudes towards doubt and questioning. Model a balanced approach by showing that faith and intellect are not mutually exclusive. Embrace both scripture and science, reason and revelation, as complimentary tools given to us by God to understand the world He created.

Scriptural engagement can provide a powerful backdrop for these conversations. Use passages that demonstrate how heroes of the faith dealt with their own questions and uncertainties. Such biblical stories can be both reassuring and instructive, showing that God's revelations often come through a journey of questioning and seeking.

Remember to tailor your responses to be age-appropriate. Simple, truthful answers are suitable for young children, while older children and teens may require more in-depth discussions. They might benefit from outside resources, such as Christian apologetics, which can help them to engage with tougher questions about faith and rationality.

When helping your child traverse spiritual doubt, be sure to reinforce the importance of prayer. Prayer is a powerful way for them to bring their uncertainties before God and seek personal insight. Cultivate a family culture where prayer is seen as a first-line response to any life challenge.

Encourage your child to maintain a journal to express their questions, discoveries, and feelings about faith. This practice can provide a reflective space for them to see how their understanding of God grows over time and how previous doubts were addressed.

Influence their critical thinking by guiding them on how to weigh evidence, discern truth, and understand different perspectives. While we are called to have faith, we are also encouraged to seek knowledge and understanding. Teaching your children how to critically process information can help them make informed decisions.

Create a safe environment for your child to express their doubts openly. If they feel that they will be judged or dismissed, they may withdraw and seek answers from less reliable or non-Christian sources. Affirm your household as a haven for honest dialogue about faith.

At times, invite a community of believers into these conversations. A mentorship from a mature Christian outside the immediate family can often offer an alternative perspective that resonates with your child. We are reminded that the body of Christ is diverse and that each member has unique insights to offer.

Lastly, use praise and worship as a means of renewing faith in moments of doubt. Music, prayer, and worship can touch the heart in ways that words sometimes cannot, and they often bring comfort and clarity in the midst of uncertainty.

Handling difficult questions and doubts with compassion and clarity is not just about giving answers. It's about walking alongside your child, as they learn to navigate the intricate path of faith, growth, and understanding. In doing so, you help to forge a foundation of discernment and trust in the Lord that will sustain your child throughout their life.

Chapter 4:
Building a Resilient Christian Family

Upon laying the foundation of love, faith, and open communication within your household, we venture into the fortitude of your kinship, sculpting a resilient Christian family that stands strong amid life's tempests. The journey of togetherness within a Christian home is embellished with worship, an unyielding faith during trials, and shared jubilations in accomplishments. As parents and guardians, your role transitions into that of an anchor and shield, allowing each moment of shared worship to become a cornerstone, unifying the family and deepening its roots in Christ. When adversities knock, it is collective faith, a tapestry woven with threads of scripture and prayers, that you wrap around your loved ones, uplifting and guiding them through challenges. Equally important is the celebration of victories, both large and small, which resonate with gratitude and acknowledge God's grace in your journey as a family. It's within these celebrations that you lay the festive stones on the path for future generations, imbuing them with the strength and joy of a faith-led life.

Strengthening Family Bonds Through Shared Worship

Within the fabric of a resilient Christian family, threads of shared worship intertwine to strengthen the unit, shaping an intimately bonded community centered on faith. This shared worship is not merely a routine, but a profound, connective practice that bathes the family in the light of spirituality and understanding.

When families come together to worship, they establish an unspoken language of love and reverence for God. This shared language allows each member, from the youngest to the oldest, to participate in the sacred act of glorifying the Creator. Each voice lifted in prayer, each hand folded in devotion, adds to the chorus of familial unity that echoes into daily life.

Gathering as a family in prayer isn't just about speaking to God; it's about listening. Through worship, God's word and wisdom permeate the heart, offering guidance and solace. In these sacred moments, the rushing noise of the world fades, allowing a family to commune in peace and grasp what truly matters.

It is said that families who pray together, stay together, and this adage holds a profound truth. As parents, including your children in the act of worship instills in them a sense of belonging to something greater than themselves. It's an experience that shapes their perspective on life, helping them to understand their place in God's grand design.

Yet, shared worship goes beyond prayer. It is found in the small rituals, the bedtime Bible stories, the grace said at dinner, and the hymns sung during household chores. Each act is a golden thread in the tapestry of a Christian family, weaving spirituality into the mundane, transforming it into something divine.

Communal worship also provides a foundation for resilience. When troubles assail your family, it is this unshakable foundation that you will return to for strength. Just as a lighthouse offers guidance through stormy seas, the light of your collective faith will guide you through life's challenges.

This foundation is laid brick by brick, as you celebrate the Lord's day together. Whether it's attending church, reading scripture, or serving the community, collective engagement in these activities fosters a sense of commitment and shared purpose within the family.

Let's not forget that worship is also joyful. As a family, creating joy in worship can be transformative. This might look like an impromptu dance to your favorite gospel song, or perhaps laughter as you share what you're grateful for. In joy, the spirit of God breathes lightness into your relationships, knitting hearts closer with cords of merriment.

For parents, shared worship offers a chance to lead by example. As your children observe your earnest devotion, they learn the importance of faith and its practice. This observation becomes the soil in which the seeds of their own spiritual journeys take root, nourished by the steady waters of family tradition and love.

In the silence of sacred space, shared worship calls for introspection and confession, essential elements for spiritual growth. A family that confesses and forgives together learns to navigate the complexities of human relationships with grace and understanding. Here, in the presence of each other, vulnerabilities are shared, and collective healing begins.

Worship also connects your family's story to the greater narrative of God's people. Through reciting the same prayers and celebrating the same holy days as countless generations before, your family joins a timeless continuum of faith. This understanding of being part of something larger brings a sense of identity and legacy that can empower each member.

Involving your children in planning and leading worship helps them to develop leadership skills and confidence in their spiritual lives. By assigning them roles or tasks, you show that their contribution is valuable, guiding them to take ownership of their faith journey.

Ultimately, the essence of shared worship within the family is transformational love. It is this love that fuels the resilient Christian family, allowing it to thrive and grow in harmony. Embodying the love of Christ within the home creates an environment where each person is cherished and teachings of the Bible are lived out daily.

When the worship ends, the echoes of it should reverberate in the kind words, the patient manner, and the gentle strength that characterize your family's interactions. This atmosphere of continual worship encourages a lifestyle where faith naturally infuses all aspects of living, creating a beacon of hope and light to all who encounter it.

By embracing shared worship as the heartbeat of your family life, you set the rhythm for a dance of love and commitment that honors God. It orchestrates a symphony of souls in harmony, empowered to face the world not just as individuals, but as a united force rooted in Christ. This is the essence of a resilient Christian family, and the seeds you plant through shared worship will bear fruit for generations to come.

Overcoming Challenges with Collective Faith

In the pursuit of building a resilient Christian family, one must recognize that every family, like a well-sailed ship, will encounter storms. The tempests of life test not only the strength of individual members but the collective faith that binds them together. It is in these turbulent times that faith serves as the most crucial anchor, one that can keep the family steadfast and united.

When faced with challenges beyond our control, whether they be financial hardships, health crises, or personal losses, it is our faith that provides solace and perspective. In these trying moments, families are invited to come together in prayer, to lay their troubles at the feet of the Divine and to seek guidance and support that transcends worldly resources.

It's important to understand that collective faith does not mean uniform faith. Each family member may experience and express their spirituality differently. Adolescents, for instance, may question and challenge as a natural part of their development. Embrace these variations, knowing that faith can thrive within diversity when it's fostered with patience and communication. It is vital that families learn to navigate these differences with grace, recognizing that each person's journey contributes to the larger tapestry of the family's shared belief.

Sharing testimonies can be immensely powerful in a family setting. When each member relays personal accounts of faith overcoming obstacles, it lays down bricks in the foundation of collective belief. These stories become part of the family lore, lessons that can inspire and fortify others in times of doubt.

One of the most practical expressions of collective faith is the establishment of a routine for prayer and worship. When the waters are calm, these routines build the muscle memory of turning toward God. When storms hit, it becomes almost instinctual for the family to gather and seek comfort and direction through these established patterns of faith.

The practice of family devotion can be a lifeline during challenges. Creating a safe space where each member can voice their concerns and place them within the context of scripture provides encouragement. It reinforces the understanding that no one in the family stands alone against their trials.

As parents, it's imperative to demonstrate unwavering faith, especially during periods of distress. Children will look to their parents as models of how to react to life's adversities. Modeling trust in God's plan and timing, even when the path is obscured, teaches resilience through faith.

Forgiveness is another cornerstone of overcoming challenges with collective faith. Misunderstandings and conflicts are inevitable in familial relationships, but forgiveness is the balm that heals wounds and restores unity. Encourage a culture of forgiveness, with the understanding that to err is human and to forgive is divine.

Intentionally seek out scriptural examples of perseverance and deliverance. The stories from the Bible serve not only as moral lessons but also as evidence of God's unwavering faithfulness in our struggles. Reflect on the trials of Job, the resolve of Esther, and the steadfastness of Daniel. Let these narratives echo in your family's journey.

There's profound strength in service, especially when we act as a family. Engaging in outreach allows the family to shift focus from internal challenges to the needs of others. This action, rooted in empathy and love, is a living testament to the values of Christianity and a powerful antidote to self-absorption during hard times.

Bringing faith into decision-making is essential. Encourage conversations that weigh choices against biblical principles and values. This collective analysis not only fosters wise decision-making but also reinforces the idea that God is invested in the minutiae of our lives.

Remember, resilience is not about never faltering; it's about the recovery that comes through faith. A family that prays together is more likely to stay together, emerging stronger after each challenge. Use trials as an opportunity to bond, fortify your trust in God, and reinforce your commitment to each other.

During particularly intense trials, seeking counsel can be a wise measure. God has blessed us with a community of believers, mentors, and church leaders who can provide guidance, support, and an outside perspective. They can bring words of wisdom and comfort that resonate deeply, aiding the family in finding clarity and direction.

And finally, celebrate the victories, no matter how small. Recognize and acknowledge when the family overcomes an obstacle through faith. Doing so cements the reality that collective faith is not just about enduring challenges but also about experiencing triumphs together. These celebrations serve as vital reminders of God's faithfulness and the power of a united family in faith.

In summary, the challenge is not to avoid storms but to navigate through them with collective faith as our compass. As a family bonded by the sacred, there is no adversity too great, no night too dark, that the light of faith cannot penetrate. Hold fast to the promise that where two or three are gathered in His name, there lies tremendous power—a power that emboldens, uplifts, and ultimately overcomes.

Celebrating Victories and Milestones Together

In the heart of every resilient Christian family lies the shared joy found in celebrating victories and milestones together. These moments, both big and small, serve as ebenezers—stones of help—that remind us of God's faithfulness and provision. They offer not just a pause for reflection, but an opportunity to grow closer as a family unit aligned in faith and purpose.

Children bloom under the warmth of encouragement and recognition. Marking the fruition of their efforts with celebration not only affirms their abilities but solidifies their sense of belonging within the family. Whether it's the achievement of academic goals, spiritual milestones like baptism, or personal victories such as learning a new skill, each one is a testament to their growth and God's goodness.

Part of nurturing a Christian family involves crafting traditions that honor these milestones. Perhaps when a child memorizes a significant portion of scripture, the family could gather to listen, each member sharing a word of encouragement. Or consider a special dinner where the table is set with care, and the family prayer focuses on giving thanks for the persistence and dedication it took to reach a particular goal.

Birthdays and anniversaries are God-given rhythms of life, natural moments to pause and reflect on the year passed and the year to come. Within the Christian home, these annual markers can become times of spiritual stock-taking. They aren't just about adding a year to one's age or to a marriage; they're about celebrating the growth that has occurred and praying for guidance in the next phase of life.

Teamwork and cooperation are pillars of strength in any family, but when that family aligns their vision with God's word, a powerful dynamic emerges. Engaging in a family service project creates a shared experience of giving and a victory in itself. Achieving a goal together, like building a house for Habitat for Humanity or feeding the homeless at a local shelter, is a visible sign of Christ's love in action that deserves celebration.

Sometimes the milestones we face are unexpected, shaped by challenges or adversity. When a family member overcomes a significant obstacle, be it an illness or a personal struggle, it's an opportunity to gather and give thanks for the resilience God grants us. This can be a private moment of prayer or maybe an open invitation to friends and extended family to join in praise and thanksgiving.

Let's not forget the smaller daily and weekly victories. Completing a week of school or work, leading a friend to Christ, or showing kindness in a trying situation may not seem monumental, yet they are the fibers of our Christian walk. Acknowledging and celebrating these consistently weaves gratitude into the fabric of family life, helping everyone recognize God's hand in the day-to-day.

Academic and extracurricular achievements call for recognition within the family. Attend recitals, award ceremonies, and sports events with enthusiasm. Celebrate good report cards or progress in areas of difficulty not just with verbal praise but perhaps with a special family outing or a thoughtful gift that echoes 'well done'.

It's essential to tailor celebrations to the individual. Some children might relish a boisterous party, while others may prefer a more introspective observance. Each child is wonderfully made by our Creator, and recognizing their uniqueness in how we celebrate can affirm their individuality and their place within the family.

As important as celebrating is the act of remembrance. Documenting these milestones in family albums or journals not only serves as a keepsake but as a spiritual ledger of God's blessings. During challenging times, these records can be a source of encouragement, recalling to mind God's past faithfulness as a promise of his continued presence.

Advent and Christmas, Easter, and other Christian holidays present the perfect backdrop for special family traditions that celebrate our shared faith. These are times not just for festive meals and shared gifts but for solidifying why we celebrate these events in the first place. They are milestones of our faith, each with a profound story that when celebrated, reaffirm our family's spiritual foundation.

But let's not just wait for the victories to celebrate. The Bible teaches us to rejoice always, pray continually, and give thanks in all circumstances. This spirit of joy should be a constant in Christian families, setting a tone that life itself and the opportunity to live it in service to Christ is a continual celebration.

Lastly, inviting others to join in these milestones can extend the joy beyond the boundaries of the immediate family. Sharing your triumphs with your church family, for instance, reinforces communal bonds and allows for the broader Christian community to uplift and support you. It's a beautiful embodiment of the scripture that tells us to rejoice with those who rejoice and mourn with those who mourn.

In truth, building a resilient Christian family isn't just about weathering the storms but equally about dancing in the rain of God's blessings. Every victory, every milestone, is a brushstroke in the masterpiece of your family's story that God is painting. Embrace these moments with open hearts, and let the joy of the Lord be your strength as you celebrate life's journey together.

Chapter 5:
The Role of the Church in Family Life

Having established the blueprint for a resilient, faith-filled home, let's now discover how the church can serve as a cornerstone in your family's spiritual journey. This sacred haven offers more than just a weekly service; it's a vibrant community eager to uplift, guide, and support each member of your family. In these hallowed walls, rich lessons await, poised to enrich your children's understanding of selfless love, stewardship, and belonging. By engaging with church ministries, your family can forge meaningful connections that reinforce a faith-infused upbringing, opening doors to mentorship and peer fellowship that sing harmoniously with the values you cherish at home. As your family's roots intertwine more deeply within this spiritual soil, watch as they draw life-giving nourishment, extending a robust canopy of faith that shades every aspect of your and your children's lives.

Integrating Church Community and Fellowship

Welcome to a profound journey into the heart of the church community and its role in invigorating family life. Every vibrant family resembles a tree with deep roots, deriving strength from the fertile soil of its community. Among the gifts of the Spirit, fellowship is a divine tapestry woven through the lives of individuals and families alike, supporting and enriching their collective spiritual journey.

The church is more than a mere building or a weekly service; it's a living, breathing community where the heartbeats of many synchronize to the rhythm of shared faith and collective purpose.

Integrating your family into this body can provide an invaluable cornerstone for growth and support. Here, you and your children can develop relationships that mirror the ones Jesus shared with his disciples—relationships steeped in love, learning, and mutual edification.

Fellowship in the church presents an opportunity for families to engage with one another in meaningful ways, from sharing meals during community gatherings to offering each other support during life's trials and triumphs. This communal tapestry fosters resilience, understanding that we are not alone in our struggles nor in our celebrations. As your family creates bonds within the church, these relationships can often become extensions of your kin, vital to the nurturing of children within a broad, compassionate network.

One of the first steps towards integrating into the church community involves regular attendance and participation in services and events. In these gatherings, your family won't just be observers but active participants in a larger story. By attending, you proclaim a willingness to be involved in the lives of others, opening doors to reciprocal involvement in your own family's journey.

Volunteering together can serve as a powerful means of fostering connectedness while imitating Christ's servant attitude. This may manifest as helping out at church events, supporting outreach programs, or contributing to the maintenance of the church facilities. By serving alongside each other, family members can experience a sense of accomplishment and witness the tangible results of their faith in action.

Church-sponsored small groups or home cells can be another avenue for deepening relationships within the community. These settings offer a chance for intimate sharing, prayer, and mutual support. They encourage a transparency and honesty that larger gatherings might not always afford, and this environment can be especially conducive to discussing the challenges and rewards of Christian parenting.

Developing mentorship relationships with seasoned believers in the church can offer additional layers of guidance and wisdom. Elders in faith can share experiences and offer reinforcement in the parenting strategies you choose. They may provide insights drawn from their reservoirs of knowledge that help illuminate the path your family treads.

Participating in church educational programs, such as Sunday School or Bible study groups, offers both you and your children the opportunity to grow in knowledge and understanding of scripture in a collaborative environment. Such settings encourage questions, foster dialogue, and cater to the learning of every age, building a strong scriptural foundation for the entire family.

Families that pray together in the presence of fellow believers cultivate a public testimony of their dependence on God. This act of communal prayer not only nurtures spiritual growth but also solidifies the bonds between family and church members, unifying hearts in seeking God's will and provision for their lives.

The church is an ideal platform for harnessing the diversity of spiritual gifts. It's vital for family members to identify and nurture these gifts within each other. By encouraging your children to explore their God-given abilities within the community, you're enabling them to fulfill their potential and contribute effectively to the body of Christ.

Celebrations and rituals are embedded in the life of the church. Your family's participation in holiday services, baptisms, and other rites mark the passage of time with communal milestones. These celebrations can root children in a tradition greater than themselves and infuse family memories with the joy of shared faith.

Through times of loss or hardship, the church community becomes a tangible manifestation of God's love. When one member suffers, each responds with the sort of compassion that carries families through their darkest hours. Moreover, when a family member is distant, the church can serve as a bridge, extending love and patience that reflects the heart of the Father.

Fostering an atmosphere of accountability is another benefit of integrating church fellowship. As your family weaves itself into the church tapestry, a natural accountability to church leaders and fellow believers can form. This may serve as a guide and check for your children, teaching them that their actions impact not only their own lives but the community's as well.

Family involvement in church missions projects can cultivate a broader worldview and a heart for service. Whether participating in local projects or traveling for missions trips, these experiences can instill in your children a sense of purpose and a commitment to the Great Commission that Jesus entrusted to His followers.

In conclusion, surrounding your family with a supportive church community is not an optional extra; it's essential. It enables your family to flourish spiritually, emotionally, and socially. Through this integration, you'll find resources, relationships, and revelations that will fuel your family's journey, anchoring you in a space where grace abounds and love permeates every interaction. Allow your family to be knit into the fabric of the church, and watch as the threads of fellowship strengthen the very core of your shared life in Christ.

Utilizing Church Resources for Parental Support

In our continuing exploration of the church's role in family life, it is essential to delve into the vast pool of resources that the church provides for parental support. Navigating the world of parenting can sometimes feel like traversing a complex labyrinth. It is comforting to know that you are not alone in this journey. For those who seek to raise their children with Christian values, the church stands as a beacon of guidance, community, and practical assistance.

The church isn't just a place for worship; it is a living community that offers an array of programs designed to bolster parental capabilities. Many churches offer parenting classes, workshops, or seminars that can provide essential insights into the Christian approach to raising children. These sessions are often led by individuals who not only understand the spiritual aspects of parenting but also the practical elements that come from experience and knowledge of child development.

One of the most valuable resources the church provides is counseling services. These services can be a godsend for parents who are struggling with family issues or simply need a listening ear. Christian counseling melds psychological principles with spiritual insight, thereby offering a holistic approach to solving problems. With compassionate hearts and discerning spirits, counselors can guide you through tough times, always pointing you back to the stalwart truths of the faith.

Moreover, the church is not just a source of wisdom for parents; it is also a place where children can find mentors. Youth pastors and Sunday school teachers play a crucial role in shaping the lives of young people by providing guidance, support, and strong role models outside of the immediate family. These individuals can be instrumental in reinforcing the values you instill at home, in a context that may resonate more deeply with your growing children.

Support groups are another cornerstone of the church's parental support system. Some churches offer groups specifically for single parents, step-families, or parents of children with special needs. These groups provide a space for sharing experiences, offering mutual support, and realizing that other families face similar challenges. There is a profound comfort in fellowship that comes from shared experiences and the collective pursuit of godly parenting.

Do not overlook the value of intergenerational relationships that the church community fosters. Elders in the faith often serve as ad hoc grandparents or wise sages to younger families, offering time-tested advice or simply a non-judgmental space to vent and seek solace. Their experiences can serve as beacons that light the way for the next generation of parents.

Church libraries or resource centers often stock books, audio, and video materials on parenting. These resources can be handy when searching for new strategies or needing encouragement. Most of these materials are selected with spiritual nourishment in mind, ensuring that their content aligns with Christian values and principles.

Service and mission opportunities provided by the church are not only for adults but can be immensely formative for children too. Participating in these activities together as a family can strengthen your bond and offer real-life examples of putting faith into action. It also presents a chance for parents to serve alongside their children, opening discussions on the importance of servitude, compassion, and living a mission-oriented life.

Financial guidance is yet another realm where churches are equipped to aid families. From budgeting workshops to stewardship seminars, churches can help parents establish sound financial practices. These principles don't just keep your household fiscal matters in order; they also teach children about responsibility, generosity, and the power of financial freedom for God-centered endeavors.

A significant facet of the church's resources for parents is the availability of childcare during services and events. By providing a safe and nurturing environment for children, parents can engage more fully with their spiritual growth and church community. Churches often have protocols in place to ensure safety and care, allowing you peace of mind while you take this time for spiritual replenishment.

Remember that the church is a collective of individuals with diverse talents and abilities. Often, you'll find that fellow church members who are educators, physicians, or seasoned parents are more than willing to share their expertise. Don't hesitate to reach out and inquire, as these informal exchanges can be just as enriching as organized programs.

For those times when you simply need to refuel spiritually, most churches offer retreats or prayer groups. These opportunities can provide the necessary pause from the daily demands of parenting, allowing for reflection, rejuvenation, and a deeper connection with God. These moments of stillness can be rare in a parent's busy life, but they are critical for maintaining personal spiritual vitality.

Lastly, your church community is a place where your own gifts can be recognized and utilized. Perhaps you have experiences that can benefit other parents, insights that might guide them, or simply an empathetic ear for their troubles. Recognize that as you draw from the church's resources, you also have the opportunity to give back, enriching the fabric of communal support.

In conclusion, the church is a reservoir of parental support that goes well beyond its spiritual mandate. It offers educational resources, counseling, interpersonal relationships, and practical assistance that can significantly ease the parental load. Tap into this support, participate actively in the church life, and watch as your family not only survives but thrives in the grace that such community fosters.

As we strive to incorporate the church's resources into our parenting practices, let us do so with humility, eagerness to learn, and a spirit of service. In this way, we become conduits for God's love and wisdom, both within our families and within the larger church community.

Engaging in Church Missions as a Family

When we consider the kaleidoscope of experiences that can enrich our family's spiritual journey, engaging in church missions stands brightly as a path of transformation. Embarking on such a mission is more than just a commitment; it's an adventure that fuses faith with action, one that can set a family on a shared path of discovery, service, and spiritual growth. In this pivotal role, the church becomes a hub, not only for worship but for active engagement in the wider community and beyond.

Why should a family venture together into missions organized by their church? Missions provide a tangible way to live out the gospel message of love and service. It reflects the heart of faith into the world and brings us closer to understanding the needs of our brothers and sisters, local and global. As a family, working in missions can bind you with threads of shared endeavours, sharpening your focus on what truly matters - being the hands and feet of Jesus in a world that yearns for touch and movement.

Consider how involvement in a mission can nurture each member of your family in unique, yet cohesive ways. Children can absorb lessons of empathy and compassion as they witness how small acts can make large ripples in someone's life. Parents can gain a deeper humility and patience while leading by example, showing their children that faith is active and practical, not merely theoretical. Missions ignite conversations about love, sacrifice, and the joy of living for others, lessons that are more potent in action than in words alone.

Yet, before setting foot on the mission field, it is crucial to prepare as a unit. Gather and pray, seeking God's guidance on where and how your family can serve best. Aligning your mission with your family's strengths and spiritual gifts not only ensures a more fruitful experience but also ensures that each member can contribute meaningfully. Whether it's a local food drive, an overseas building project, or supporting church planters, each mission will offer unique challenges and rewards.

While serving, keep in mind that flexibility and a servant's heart are key. With a multitude of needs and uncertainties, missions often involve stepping out of comfort zones. As a family, you'll learn to adapt, to support one another, and to find resilience in your collective faith. This adaptability is valuable not only on the mission field but in all spheres of life where the unexpected becomes the norm.

As for young ones, engaging in church missions can construct a foundation of lifelong service. It offers a real-world context for the biblical principles they learn, turning Sunday teachings into weekday actions. Children and teenagers who serve alongside their parents are often inspired to take initiative, to see beyond their needs, to grasp the profound simplicity of giving.

And what of the bonds forged during these shared experiences? They can be deep and enduring. Missions can cultivate a family dynamic centered on cooperation. As you work towards common goals, the sense of unity and purpose can bring a new dimension to your relationships. There is a certain joy found in communal achievements, particularly when they are sown in spiritual soil.

One cannot overlook the personal spiritual growth that comes from mission work. As each family member encounters new people and situations, they are often moved to reflect inwardly, to question and to seek. This self-reflection is fertile ground for growth, inviting us to assess where we've been, where we're going, and how our faith directs our journey.

Upon returning from a mission, it's natural to experience a range of emotions and a shift in perspective. Re-entry can bring its own set of challenges as you try to integrate all that you've learned and experienced into daily life. It's important to debrief as a family and share openly about what you've witnessed. Share the highs and the struggles, and discuss how what you've learned can be woven into the fabric of your daily existence.

To take it further, encourage each family member to consider how the mission has impacted them personally. Has it clarified a sense of calling or opened up new avenues for service? Has it altered the way they perceive their neighbors, both near and far? Such reflections solidify the mission's impact, carving lessons and memories into hearts and minds.

The communal aspect of church missions isn't to be underestimated. Engaging with others from your church family or partnering with another organization creates an extended support network. It builds relationships that cross the lines of age, culture, and background, enriching your family's social world and offering diverse role models for your children.

Ultimately, church missions shape a family's legacy. They become part of your shared story, a testament to a time when you stepped out together in faith. These stories, colored with personal anecdotes and spiritual insights, are passed down, encouraging others and perpetuating a heritage of service and faithfulness.

In conclusion, embarking on church missions as a family is an invitation to a deeper faith experience. It's a challenge, a lesson, and an opportunity all rolled into one. As your family serves, learns, and grows through missions, remember that every action, however small it may seem, is a stitch in the tapestry of God's grand design, a design that you're blessed to contribute to as a family united in service and love.

Chapter 6:
Education and Christian Values

As we delve into the heart of education, embarking on a journey shadowed with both light and shade, understanding how to integrate Christian values into this essential realm becomes not just beneficial but vital for our children's spiritual armor. Navigating educational paths requires wisdom, and it's our responsibility to illuminate each step with God's Word. When selecting schools or academic resources, we're tasked with ensuring that these environments can either complement or be complemented by the biblical truths we hold dear. In a world where secular and spiritual perspectives often clash, we must equip our youngsters with the discernment to reconcile their faith with seemingly contrary worldviews, without succumbing to them. It's about fostering an unwavering foundation in Christ while cultivating a robust intellect that can engage, challenge, and transform the marketplace of ideas they will inevitably encounter. This balance allows them to not just survive but thrive as informed Christians, shaping rather than being shaped by the culture around them.

Choosing the Right Education Path

As we continue our journey understanding the integration of Christian values in family life, we arrive at a crossroads that captures the essence of stewardship and guidance – education. The path your child embarks upon in their educational pursuit is pivotal, not just academically but spiritually as well. Choosing the right education path intersects with our core aspirations to instill Christian fundamentals within our children.

Education is a veritable vessel that carries not only knowledge but beliefs, attitudes, and a framework for understanding the world. Embarking on this path, our intrinsic duty as parents is to consider the whole child - their mind, body, and spirit. Thus, the significance of selecting an education route congruent with our Christian ethos cannot be overstated.

An education steeped in Christian values doesn't only imbue a sense of ethical discipline but positions our children to view their studies through the lens of faith. It is a harmonious blending of intellectual growth with spiritual enrichment. Your child's learning environment should reflect the morals that resonate within your family and echo the voice of Scripture.

Conversation around the kitchen table about schools should involve prayers for discernment. Consider what the Bible teaches about wisdom, understanding, and knowledge. Reflect upon Proverbs 22:6, "Train up a child in the way he should go: and when he is old, he will not depart from it." Deciphering this in the context of education prompts us to evaluate schools that don't merely teach to the test but to the heart.

An essential step in this process is visiting potential schools, meeting with educators, and evaluating curricula through a Christ-centered perspective. Are the teachings compatible with your family's beliefs? Will your child be fortified with courage to stand firm in their faith amidst a tapestry of diverse thoughts?

This doesn't necessitate a disregard for secular education; rather, it calls for vigilance and engagement. The ability to integrate biblical truths into daily learning is a skill that Christian education can cultivate – preparing our children to transform societies, not be conformed to them.

Moreover, let's not overlook the importance of integrating faith with reason. A well-rounded Christian education encourages critical thinking, grounded in a foundation of faith that points towards truth. This is not just about learning Scripture, but about fostering an analytical mind that filters through life's complexities with the wisdom of the Word.

For some families, the best choice might be home education, where parents have a direct hand in shaping the curriculum and ensuring that the lessons are imbued with Christian virtues. Perhaps this is a path that aligns with your family's dynamic, nurturing the faith journey within the intimacy of your home.

Others might seek out Christian schools that align with denominational beliefs or those that simply center Christ in their teaching. The camaraderie of like-minded peers can reinforce the values you teach at home, fostering a collective environment of faith-based growth. Do not hesitate to pursue these options if they resonate with your family's faith goals.

Moreover, if the chosen path is a public or secular private school, involvement and advocacy for your child's spiritual needs remains paramount. This doesn't end with taking a backseat but involves active participation in your child's education. Engage with teachers, administrators, and even school boards to understand how your child's Christian perspective will be considered and respected in their educational journey.

It's vital to provide reinforcement at home, where discussions about classroom experiences can be had in the light of biblical principles. This dual engagement in school and at home will arm your child with the tools to navigate a secular educational experience while maintaining their Christian integrity.

Supplementing education with extracurricular activities rooted in your church community, Christian youth groups, and Bible studies also fortifies your child's ability to synthesize their faith with their learning. Such activities not only offer additional educational enrichment but provide a community of support, echoing the values taught at home and in church.

In all these considerations, remember that the education path for your child is not set in stone but is instead a journey with thoughtful stops and starts. Regular reassessment and openness to change are crucial as your child grows and your family's needs evolve. Keep your heart and mind open to God's leading; He may surprise you with the doors He opens and the paths He illuminates.

Finally, let's address the heart of the matter – education is a gift from God, and within this gift is the potential to shape a soul for His glory. Your involvement in your child's education reveals your commitment to stewarding that gift thoughtfully, reflecting God's purpose for your child. Let every educational step be taken with the prayer that it leads your child closer to God and further into His divine wisdom.

As we wrap up this section, take heart in knowing that the process of choosing the right education path for your child is an act of love, illuminated by prayer and grounded in the truth of the gospel. Your efforts lay the foundation for a future where your child, educated and influenced by faith, can emerge as a beacon of Christ's light in the world.

Promoting Biblical Truths in Learning

In the ongoing pursuit of raising children with a strong moral foundation, it is essential to place the Word of God at the heart of their education. For parents dedicated to this mission, it is a journey filled with both challenge and profound reward. Faith, after all, is not reserved for Sundays alone but is meant to be woven into the very fabric of our daily lives, including the education of our young ones.

Education, when centered on biblical truths, becomes more than just academic learning—it transforms into life learning, where knowledge of Scriptures and Christian values guides your child's understanding of the world around them. It starts within the home, where parents can serve as primary educators of faith. Consider beginning each day with a morning prayer or a verse from the Bible that sets a tone of thankfulness and reflection. This simple act reminds children that all wisdom ultimately flows from the divine.

The task then extends to the selection of educational resources. Encourage your children's curiosity by integrating biblically based books, videos, and activities into their learning. Choose materials that not only educate but also illuminate biblical principles. For example, when teaching history, highlight individuals who have shown exemplary faith or use stories from the Bible to illustrate moral lessons embedded within historical contexts.

Furthermore, help your children recognize the presence of God's hand in all creation. When studying science, point out the complexity and beauty of the world, which speaks to the intricate design by an intelligent Creator. By doing so, children learn to appreciate not only the physical laws but also the spiritual truths that govern our existence.

In mathematics, teach the value of honesty and precision; these are qualities esteemed in Christian character and are instrumental when dealing with numbers and critical thinking. Encourage your children to see the reliability of mathematics as a reflection of the orderliness of God's universe.

When it comes to literature, choose stories that epitomize moral courage, redemption, and truth. Discuss characters and plots through the lens of Scripture, asking questions like, "How does this character's journey reflect the values we hold dear?" or "What can we learn from their choices and the consequences that follow?"

Engaging in the arts is another powerful way to promote biblical truths. Creation itself is an art form, and children should be encouraged to express their understanding and adoration of God's work through their creativity. Whether it's through drawing, painting, music, or drama, the arts offer a profound means to reflect God's beauty and convey His messages of love and hope.

An equally important aspect of learning is encouraging discussions around biblical truths. As children grow and encounter various worldviews, it is vital for parents to engage in open and compassionate conversations about what they learn. Ask them about their thoughts and feelings on school topics and compare them to what the Scriptures teach. This practice helps children articulate their faith and solidify it amidst diverse perspectives.

Do not shy away from difficult questions or doubts your child may express. Instead, use these moments to delve deeper into God's Word together, seeking answers and understanding. It's important to reassure them that faith does not fear inquiry but rather invites exploration and growth.

Field trips and educational excursions offer practical ways to apply biblical truths. Visiting museums, parks, and historical sites provides an avenue for children to witness the breadth of God's creation and the flow of human history within His providential care. Use these trips as opportunities to discuss the integration of faith and learning in real-world scenarios.

Within the classroom, if the school environment is secular, advocate for respect towards Christian perspectives and encourage your child to also respect differing views. Help them understand that God's love and truth extend to all people, regardless of their beliefs, and that they can be a positive influence by showing grace and understanding.

In addition to formal education, don't overlook the importance of informal learning environments. Your child's involvement in church activities, youth groups, and biblical studies enriches their knowledge and love for God. These spaces allow for fellowship and deeper engagement with peers who share similar values.

Lastly, pray for your child's intellectual and spiritual growth. Trust that God will grant them discernment, wisdom, and favor throughout their educational journey. Remember that promoting biblical truths in learning is not just a parental responsibility but also a divine cooperation. As you plant and water the seeds of faith within your child, it is God who will bring the increase (1 Corinthians 3:7).

The pursuit of promoting biblical truths in learning can be the most rewarding part of your parenting journey. It's about being present, prepared, and prayerful as you guide your child through an education that is deeply rooted in faith. Let the light of God's Word lead them to true wisdom that endures beyond school years, shaping them into individuals ready to live a life that honors and reflects Christ.

With every lesson grounded in Scripture, every discovery framed by faith, and every question met with biblical wisdom, you are crafting not just a scholar but a disciple. This is your calling as a Christian parent, and it is a higher education that prepares your child for eternity as much as for earthly success. Your efforts invest in a legacy that will bear fruit for generations to come, as your children learn to walk in the light of God's truth and love.

Dealing With Contrary Worldviews in Secular Education

In the pursuit of raising children grounded in Christian values, one of the most challenging arenas we encounter is secular education. Within the halls of public schools and many private institutions, our children are exposed to an array of worldviews that can often contradict the faith-based principles we cherish. As they embark on their educational journey, we are called to equip and fortify them with wisdom, understanding, and the courage to stand firm in their beliefs.

The academic environment is a mosaic of thoughts and philosophies, and while diversity of thought is an essential part of learning, it can also pose complex questions for our children. Preparing them to navigate these waters requires open dialogue. We must embrace the conversations that come from exposure to different beliefs and use them as opportunities to reinforce the Christian worldview with compassion and reason.

One of the first steps in this preparation is understanding that knowledge and faith need not be at odds. Encourage your children to excel academically while seeing God's hand in all forms of truth and beauty. Reinforce that learning can deepen their faith, as all truth ultimately comes from God, irrespective of the source it's presented from.

Engage with your children about what they're learning. Ask questions and show genuine interest, not only to monitor their education but to connect their experiences back to the teachings of Christ. In doing so, you provide a safe space for them to voice their thoughts and uncertainties.

As they face differing perspectives, instill in them both the humility to listen and the discernment to sift through what aligns with their faith. Teach them that Christ calls us to love and respect all people, even when we disagree with their viewpoints. In this way, we can turn potential conflicts into lessons of grace and understanding.

Strengthening their critical thinking is also essential. Let them know it's okay to question and seek answers. This practice doesn't weaken faith; it fortifies it by building a foundation that isn't easily shaken because it's been thoroughly examined and understood.

As parents, being involved in their educational choices is key. This means not only selecting the right school when possible but also advocating for your child's right to express their faith. It can mean requesting alternative assignments if content conflicts with Christian values, or helping them to constructively express their perspective in assignments and discussions.

Equip them with a biblical understanding of tolerance and love. The Christian concept of love doesn't preclude standing up for one's beliefs—rather, it commands we speak the truth in love. This can help your child approach discussions not as debates to win, but as opportunities to share the hope and joy found in Christ.

Encourage them to find fellowship with like-minded peers. Whether through a youth group, a Christian club at their school, or community service, these connections can provide support and encouragement, reinforcing their faith amidst a cacophony of worldviews.

Remember that doubts and questions are a natural part of a maturing faith. When your child expresses doubts, don't react with fear or disappointment. Use these moments to explore their thoughts, going deeper into the reasoning behind Christian beliefs and acknowledging the complexities of life and spirituality.

Model how to live unapologetically in faith while still being a respectful and responsible citizen and student. Your own example is the most powerful tool in teaching your child. When they see you engaging with the world from a place of faith-filled confidence, they learn to do the same.

Pray with and for your child, entrusting them to God's guidance every day. Prayer is your most enduring and intimate source of strength. It is the bedrock upon which you and your child can stand when faced with challenges to your faith.

Finally, recognize that your child is God's first. While we strive to guide them, ultimately their journey is between them and the Lord. Trusting God with your child's heart is an act of faith in and of itself, one that honors Him and teaches your child to do the same.

Armed with love, knowledge, and unwavering faith, our children can not only navigate a secular education but also shine as beacons of God's light within it. In doing so, they become living testimonies to the enduring power and relevance of Christian values in an ever-changing world.

Take heart, for this is not a journey you walk alone. The Holy Spirit is a guide and counselor for you and your children, providing the wisdom and discernment needed at every turn. Stand firm in faith, and watch as your children grow into thoughtful, well-educated ambassadors for Christ. Amen.

Chapter 7:
Discipline with Purpose and Love

In the previous chapters, we've laid the foundation for a home where love and faith freely ripple through each interaction. As we transition into this crucial chapter, remember that discipline isn't just about correction, but about shaping the soul with intention and tenderness. In "Discipline with Purpose and Love," the focus is to merge the gentle warmth of love with the steadfast structure of purpose. Discover how to apply disciplinary measures that honor God's teachings and respect your child's burgeoning spirit. The essence of Godly discipline is found not in the mere act of setting rules, but in nurturing a profound understanding of right and wrong within your child's heart. Approach discipline as an opportunity to guide your children towards a path of self-discipline and moral strength—a journey where they learn consequences and wisdom under the steadying hand of your patient love. With each trailing moment of guidance, we're sculpting our children's character with loving precision—affirming their worth, fortifying their conscience, and steadily pointing them towards the light of God's undying love and enduring wisdom.

Understanding Biblical Disciplinary Principles

At the heart of disciplined parenting is the Biblical directive: "Train up a child in the way he should go: and when he is old, he won't depart from it" (Proverbs 22:6 KJV). This poignant verse encapsulates the enduring responsibility placed upon us as parents to guide our children not just through correction, but through comprehensive spiritual formation. Within these next few paragraphs, we'll embark upon a journey of understanding the principles that underpin Biblical discipline, viewing them as the fibers that weave together a tapestry of godly upbringing.

In the scope of Biblical teaching, discipline isn't merely about correction, but about a holistic approach to nurturing the spirit and character of the child. It is purposeful and stems from a place of unyielding love. To understand this, one must look at the nature of God's discipline towards us, His children. "For whom the Lord loves He chastens" (Hebrews 12:6 NKJV), illustrating that discipline is a facet of love, not separate from it.

It's essential to recognize that discipline in a Biblical sense is proactive, rather than purely reactive. It involves setting boundaries and expectations clearly and with love from the onset. This preemptive strategy paves a clear path for our young ones, helping them to understand their boundaries within the safety net of parental guidance and God's word.

Reflecting on the story of Solomon's wisdom, we can see the value placed on discernment in discipline. Solomon's heart sought understanding to "discern between good and bad" (1 Kings 3:9 NKJV). As parents, our discipline should be tempered with such discernment to tailor our approach to each child's unique spirit and personal growth journey.

Discipline should always be measured and appropriate, echoing the Apostle Paul's counsel, "Fathers, provoke not your children to wrath: but bring them up in the nurture and admonition of the Lord" (Ephesians 6:4 KJV). The purpose is not to exasperate or discourage, but to uplift and guide within a framework of respect and reverence.

The parables Jesus taught provide valuable insight into the manner in which we should approach correction. They often involve principles of justice tempered with grace, reflecting the balance needed in parental discipline. As we hold our children accountable, we must also embrace forgiveness and redemption, crucial aspects of their spiritual and moral foundation.

Moreover, Biblical discipline is consistent. The book of Numbers speaks to the importance of consistency in upholding God's principles, as it recounts the consequences faced by the Israelites when they veered off the path. Consistency in discipline helps children understand the reliability of consequences and the stability of their family structure.

In the fabric of Biblical teachings, communication stands as a key principle. The Proverbs are replete with references to the power of words and the necessity for imparting wisdom through our speech. Joyful hearts and a gentle tongue are the tools with which we should construct our words of discipline, ensuring our guidance is comprehensible and imbued with love.

It's also vital that we lend an ear to understand the grievances and perspectives of our children. As the Bible implores us to be quick to hear and slow to speak (James 1:19), a similar approach in discipline fosters an environment where children feel heard and validated, even in the midst of correction.

Consequences within Biblical discipline are logical and directly related to the action requiring correction. Just as the Old Testament law tied consequences directly to actions, so too should our parental discipline help children connect their choices with outcomes, teaching responsibility and the nature of consequence in a real and tangible way.

Compassion is a cornerstone of discipline within the Bible. In the same way that Christ showed compassion to those around Him, we must let compassion guide our disciplinary efforts. This mirrors the heart of God, who is rich in mercy and whose loving-kindness is steadfast and ever-present.

The ultimate goal of Biblical discipline is restoration and growth, not punishment. Just as Jesus restored Peter after his denial, we too should aim to restore and build up our children, even when they falter. It's about steering them back onto the right path with gentle guidance that reflects God's grace.

Humility in disciplining is key to maintaining the right perspective. We must acknowledge before God and our children that we too are fallible, following David's example who was a man after God's own heart, yet acknowledged his own shortcomings. In doing so, we create an atmosphere of mutual respect and continuous learning.

As we traverse the journey of parenting, let us grasp the biblical principle that discipline is an act of hope. It anticipates the growth, the maturity, and the fruit that will come from those temporarily challenging moments. It beholds the potential within each child, cultivating it with patience and faithfulness.

In closing this exploration of Biblical disciplinary principles, remember that the rod of discipline is not solely about correction but metaphorically represents guidance, leading, and the shepherd's care that protects and nurtures. Our role is not dissimilar to the shepherd's, as we watch over our children with both a rod and a staff of comfort. Let's embrace these principles with the assurance that as we apply them with wisdom, they'll yield peaceable fruit — well-adjusted, morally-strong individuals who navigate life's complexities with a deeply rooted knowledge of God's ways.

Appropriate Discipline Techniques for Different Ages

As we journey through the realm of purposeful and loving discipline, it's crucial to recognize that each age presents its own unique challenges and opportunities. The way we guide and correct our young ones must evolve with their growing hearts and minds, ensuring that the seeds of discipline are deeply rooted in love and intentionality.

For toddlers, discipline begins with boundaries that are both clear and full of compassion. It is during the tender years of 1-3 that simple yet firm directives pave the way for understanding right from wrong. Gently redirecting behavior, coupled with a soothing voice, instills a sense of security within those small but spirited souls. Encouragement for desired behavior goes a long way in nurturing a sense of accomplishment and self-regulation.

Moving on to preschoolers, aged 4 to 5, the canvas of communication expands. These young children thrive on routines and predictability, which serve as guideposts for behavior. Providing choices within boundaries empowers them, affirming their growing independence while maintaining discipline. It's a dance between parental guidance and allowing natural consequences to teach valuable lessons, always swaying to the rhythm of understanding and empathy.

With school-aged children, age 6 to 12, our approach to discipline can be more collaborative. This is the age where discussions can bear fruit, where reasoning can take hold in fertile minds. Consequences should be relevant and logical, flowing from their actions as naturally as the consequence of a seed taking root and sprouting. Consistent rules reinforced with love affirm a sense of justice and integrity within their emerging values.

The pre-teen years, on the brink of adolescence, test the waters of autonomy and identity. For 13 to 14-year-olds, discipline should pivot towards respectful negotiation and increased responsibility. As they strive to define themselves, we must stand firm yet be willing to listen, to give and take. When discipline is necessary, it should resonate with their growing desire for adult respect, using time apart for reflection rather than punitive isolation.

Diving headlong into the teenage years, young individuals aged 15 to 18 yearn for freedom yet long for guidance. Discipline at this stage should be forward-looking, emphasizing the consequences their current choices have on their future selves. Holding them accountable in a way that mirrors the adult world applauds their emerging maturity. Mentorship replaces direct discipline, as mutual respect becomes the cornerstone of behavioral expectations.

It bears mentioning that consistency is the thread that binds all these techniques. A steady hand in discipline, one that corrects with love and certainty, teaches children at any age that they are held to a standard that won't shift with moods or circumstances. This consistency reflects God's unchanging nature and cultivates trust in His divine guidance as well.

When applying discipline, we must be attuned to each child's temperament and individuality. No single technique is a panacea, but rather, a tapestry of approaches tailored to each child's fabric. Some children respond to words, others to action, others still to quiet reflection. Discerning the difference is part of the wisdom we ask for in prayerful parenting.

Patience undergirds all discipline. The time it takes for a seed to sprout is not within our control, yet we water and tend it all the same, trusting in the eventual harvest. So too must we approach discipline with the perspective of a gentle gardener, nurturing growth over time with a calm spirit.

Let us not forget the importance of modeling the behavior we wish to see. Children are keen observers, and our actions speak to them on a profound level. Discipline should not merely be external rules imposed upon them, but a reflection of the life we live before them—the principles we embody, the love we share, and the faith we hold dear.

Rewards and praise have their place in discipline, for encouragement is the sunlight upon the soul. When children do well, a kind word or a loving gesture can make the mark of affirmation deeply felt. Just as our Heavenly Father celebrates our steps in righteousness, we too must rejoice in our children's progress.

Moreover, when we must correct, let it always be tempered with grace. Harshness can wilt tender spirits, but correction delivered with a heart of mercy can be a healing balm. We have been given the divine task of shepherding our little flocks—may we do so with hands that heal and hearts that understand.

In times where discipline seems to bear no fruit, where we feel at the end of our patience, it's paramount to lean into faith and trust that our efforts are not in vain. Even the most resilient plants face storms, but those with deep roots will stand firm. Regardless of the challenges, our steadfast commitment to discipline with purpose and love will undergird their ultimate flourishing.

Lastly, it is through prayer that we gain strength and wisdom in discipline. In those quiet moments of reflection, we are reminded that we are not alone in our parenting journey. We are co-laborers with God, shaping souls for eternity. In this partnership, we find the assurance and guidance necessary to discipline not just effectively but righteously.

As we tailor our discipline techniques to each stage of our children's development, we fulfil a calling that echoes through generations. Through conscious, loving guidance, we lay the foundation for them to grow into adults who embody integrity, compassion, and deep spiritual strength. It is indeed a journey of purpose—discipline with a love that reflects the very heart of God.

The Long-Term Impact of Consistent, Loving Discipline

The values we instill in our children shape not only their childhood but also their future generations. As gardeners of their young spirits, we must cultivate their growth with thoughtful care and consistent nurturing. In the realm of discipline, love and consistency are paramount to yielding the fruit of character that will sustain them through life's many seasons.

Within the tapestry of a Christian upbringing, the warp and weft of discipline and love create a resilient fabric to withstand the trials of life. Let us explore the enduring influence of consistent, loving discipline on a child's journey to adulthood and beyond—their relationship with God, with others, and with themselves is of eternal consequence.

When we approach discipline with a loving consistency, we lay down a path of clear expectations. These boundaries impart security and stability, allowing children to navigate the complexities of life while anchored in a sense of predictable order. As they grow older, this internal compass will guide them through moral dilemmas and social pressures, rooted in the knowledge of what is principled and true.

Consider further the role of loving discipline in the development of trust. A child raised with a reliable framework of discipline knows they are cared for and taken seriously. This trust blossoms into an invaluable ability to form healthy relationships, where mutual respect and care become cornerstones, reflecting the love of Christ in every interaction.

Patience, an oft-overlooked virtue, is also a fruit of consistent, loving discipline. Rather than responding impulsively, children learn the strength it takes to wait, endure, and persevere. They see these traits mirrored in the persistent love of their parents—and in a greater sense, in the boundless patience God extends to us all.

Paired with patience is the cultivation of self-discipline. A consistent approach in the early years bears the promise of internal self-regulation. As young adults, our children will face temptations and trials aplenty. It is the discipline ingrained within, tempered by love, that empowers them to choose the narrow path, even when wider, perilous roads beckon.

Humble accountability is yet another blessing that emerges from the well-disciplined soil. We hold our children accountable because they are precious to us, and in doing so, teach them to do the same. A soul that can bear responsibility for its actions is one that carries the light of Christ into the world, owning both its flaws and its ability to rise above them.

Love as the motivator behind discipline ensures the lesson of empathy is not lost. Witnessing discipline given in love, children learn to understand others, to step into the shoes of those around them and act with compassion. Isn't that the essence of following Jesus—developing a heart that beats with empathy and kindness for our neighbors?

Consistency models a God-like steadfastness. Children observe and eventually emulate this characteristic. They will understand that, just as their earthly parents are steadfast in their guiding principles, so is their Heavenly Father constant in His love and mercy.

Now, let us not forget resilience, a byproduct of well-seated discipline. When children are taught to rise after a fall, acknowledging the mistake but not being defined by it, they develop an indomitable spirit. As adults, their resilience enables them to weather storms, trusting in God's faithfulness and their own fortified spirits to overcome.

Self-worth tied to unconditional love, rather than transient achievements or fleeting moments of conformity, burgeons under consistently loving discipline. Children realize their value in the eyes of their parents and, ultimately, in the sight of God. They stand firm in this identity, unswayed by the world's shallow judgments.

We can't overlook the impact of discipline on a child's spiritual life. Early lessons of obedience and reverence cultivate a deep, abiding relationship with the Lord. This connection, once forged, becomes an unwavering source of guidance and solace throughout their life's journey, leading them ever closer to the heart of God.

In imparting the capacity for discernment, loving discipline also plays a crucial role. By evaluating their decisions within a well-defined moral framework, children learn to discern between right and wrong, to choose wisely, illuminating their path with the bright lantern of Biblical wisdom.

Finally, the impact ripples beyond our immediate families. Children raised in the gentle but firm hands of consistent, loving discipline become adults who contribute positively to the community. They stand as beacons of integrity and kindness, leading by example, and shaping a society that reflects heavenly ideals in earthly realms.

Loving discipline, consistent and thoughtful, is an investment into the eternal legacy of your child's character. It's an arduous task, no doubt, a continuous act of devotion and service to the potential locked within each young heart. Yet, this labor of love is what crafts legends from lives, and leaves an imprint on the world that traces back to the heart of the home—the steadfast, nurturing love of a parent, rooted in the perfect love of our Father above.

Chapter 8:
Cultivating a Life of Worship and Praise

As we step further into the realm of nurturing a home saturated with devotion, Chapter 8 invites us to immerse ourselves in the sanctifying act of worship and praise. In this sacred space, we come to recognize that worship extends beyond the walls of the church and into the very heart of family life. Here, we are called to weave a tapestry of adoration that wraps our daily routines in the warmth of God's presence. At the breakfast table, during the commute, or in the quiet twilight at day's end, the family that unites in a chorus of gratitude cultivates a profound connection with the Divine.

We discover how worship can be both a spontaneous outpouring of the heart and a deliberate practice, infusing our children's lives with a rhythm that echoes the heartbeat of faith. This chapter isn't just about standing in pews or lifting hands in song but about finding and fostering moments where the spirit of worship can resonate in the simplest of acts – a melody hummed, a sunset marveled at, or a prayer whispered in the stillness. It's there, in the interplay of the everyday and the eternal, that children learn to see their worth and their world through eyes of wonder and hearts filled with His song.

Making Worship a Daily Family Practice

Envisage worship as the heartbeat of the home—a rhythm that infuses each day with grace and unity. In elevating worship to a daily family occurrence, one not only nurtures a profound connection with the

Divine but also strengthens the bonds that tether hearts together in faith and love.

Begin by establishing a time each day dedicated to worship. This could be in the morning, where the new light ushers in a chorus of thankfulness, or in the evening, when the quiet of night allows reflection on the day's grace. Within this sacred space, integrate moments of praise, scripture reading, and prayer, crafting a mosaic of devotion that each family member contributes to.

The spontaneity of worship should be embraced as readily as its structure. Encourage children to identify and seize opportunities for worship throughout their day. A spontaneous prayer of thanks, a moment acknowledging the majesty of creation, or an impromptu conversation about God's love can weave worship naturally into the life's fabric.

Let songs of praise fill your home, creating an atmosphere of joy and reverence. Music speaks directly to the soul, imbuing the mundane with the essence of the sacred. As voices and hearts unite in song, a powerful connection to God is forged, elevating the spirit and instilling a sense of divine presence.

Scripture is the bedrock of Christian life and should be a cornerstone of daily worship. Embolden your family to immerse themselves in the Word, to live by its wisdom and to allow it to guide their actions. These sacred words are a compass, steering one's journey through life with steadfast conviction and clarity.

Integrating prayer into the ebb and flow of the day fosters a constant dialogue with the Lord. Encourage each family member to bring their aspirations, concerns, and gratitude before God, forging a personal and profound relationship with Him. Prayer becomes the whispered confidences of a child to their Creator, a source of comfort and guidance.

Consider the power of silent worship—moments of collective stillness where the family shares in the presence of the Holy Spirit. In these quietude pockets, hearts can tune into the divine frequency, receiving God's love and listening for His gentle whisper amidst life's clamor.

Worship extends beyond the walls of one's home. Urge children to find beauty in serving others, to see acts of kindness and love as worship made visible. Whether it's assisting a neighbor or caring for creation, service is a profound expression of one's love for God and commitment to a Christ-like life.

Special occasions and seasons within the Christian calendar offer unique opportunities to deepen the family's worship practice. Leverage these moments to celebrate, reflect, and cultivate an appreciation for the richness of our faith's traditions and the depth of its history.

In making room for reflection and confession within the worship practice, encourage openness and vulnerability. This fosters an environment where sins are acknowledged, forgiveness is sought, and grace is celebrated—a vital process in spiritual growth and relational healing.

As children grow, their understanding and expression of worship will evolve. Engage with them, validating their experiences and encouraging exploration. As they encounter God in ways that resonate with their burgeoning identity, they are more likely to maintain a lifelong practice of worship.

Cultivate a household where testimonies of faith are shared and valorized. When every family member voices how God's hand is moving in their life, it knits a tapestry of living faith that can inspire and bolster one another.

While structure in worship is vital, flexibility is the counterpart that allows it to flourish. Adapt practices as your family evolves, always ensuring that worship remains a source of joy and not a regimen that stifles or burdens.

Lastly, model the worship you wish to instill. Children will emulate the authenticity they observe in their parents. When they witness true reverence and delight in worship from you, they are more likely to adopt and personalize these practices. Be diligent yet gentle, constant yet creative, and always anchored in the profound love that overflows from our Father's heart.

By weaving worship into the daily life of the family, you cultivate a sanctuary of faith, a place where the presence of God is as natural as breathing. And through these practices, you not only raise children who know of the Lord but nurture souls who walk intimately with Him all the days of their lives.

Creative Expression of Faith Through Arts and Music

In the rich tapestry of Christian living, worship goes far beyond the spoken word and extends into the vibrant, emotive realms of arts and music. Imagine turning to the hymns and paintings of old, where believers of the past have laid down the riches of their hearts—faith artistically enshrined.

For families yearning to weave faith into every corner of their lives, the arts present a profound avenue. Through painting, music, dance, and theatre, you and your children can explore and express the depths of your belief in ways words often cannot capture. This exploration begins within the home, where creativity in worship is as natural as prayer.

Let's consider music first, where melody and lyrics combine in praise. Children are often drawn to the joy of song, and when you integrate worship music into your daily routines, you invite an atmosphere of reverence. You don't need to be accomplished musicians; simply allow your voices to unite in singing hymns or praise songs during your morning rituals or evening wind-down time.

Just as David played his harp and composed Psalms, encourage your young ones to learn an instrument. As they practice, guide them to offer their music as a personal act of worship. Whether clapping hands to a beat, playing a piano piece, or strumming a guitar, music becomes a powerful expression of faith that can echo through the walls of your home and into the heavens.

Visual arts, too, offer a silent yet potent medium for worship. Holding a paintbrush, a child can express their understanding of God's creation, painting the hues of a sunset or the delicate form of a flower. As they create, conversations about the Creator can organically arise, instilling a profound respect and admiration for His work.

Engaging in family art projects can become meaningful traditions. For instance, crafting a Nativity scene during Christmas time or drawing biblical scenes not only reinforces scriptural narratives but also allows for self-expression within the bounds of those stories. Every stroke, every color chosen, becomes a part of your family's unique testimony.

By attending to the inward spirit, dance and theatre in worship remain unparalleled. As your children reenact biblical stories or use dance to interpret worship songs, they physically embody their understanding of their faith. This full-bodied devotion can be deeply moving, allowing children to experience the embodiment of praise and the storytelling nature of the gospel.

In embracing these artistic expressions, it is essential to foster an environment that prioritizes joy and connection over perfection. A child's rendering of Noah's Ark need not be gallery-worthy, nor a performance of a parable Broadway-ready. What counts is the heart, the intent, and the family unity in celebrating God's presence through creativity.

Beyond fostering an individual's creativity, the arts and music offer communal experiences that enhance worship. Participating in church choirs or drama ministries helps children understand the collective aspect of faith. Learning to harmonize with others in song or cooperate in a drama team can parallel lessons in harmonizing in life and faith with the greater community.

It is also an opportunity for outreach and testimony. A child's artwork or a family's musical rendition can be a gentle bridge to share the gospel with others. Displaying these creations can open dialogue with friends and neighbors, allowing for evangelism to flow as freely as the art itself.

When your children explore the stories and themes of the Bible through art, they forge personal connections with the scriptures. They learn not just to recite verses but to visualize them, internalize them, and interpret them in ways that resonate deeply with their own spirits.

By appreciating and crafting Christian art and music, your family joins a long lineage of believers who have used these gifts to exalt their Creator. Whether it is through a spontaneous dance of joy, a painting that honors the beauty of God's earth, or a song lifted in genuine worship, your home will reverberate with a chorus of faith that honors the Lord in all His glory.

Do not underestimate the power of these forms of expression to cultivate a lasting, fervent passion for God within your children. As they grow, the seeds planted through these experiences can blossom into a vibrant, unwavering love for the Lord that is expressed in every area of their lives. And as they continue to walk in their faith, so too may they pass on this legacy of worship through the arts to future generations.

Lastly, empower your children to create with freedom and to worship without constraints. Encourage them, praise their efforts, and offer guidance gently. Let each brushstroke, each note, each movement speak its piece in the wondrous language of faith that transcends words, offering back to the Creator the beauty He has instilled within us all.

Instilling a Heart of Gratitude and Adoration for God

As we delve into nurturing a life of worship and praise, a heart full of gratitude and adoration for God stands as a bright beacon in our efforts. It is one thing to teach children about God, but to instill in them a heartfelt thankfulness and awe is a deeper, more transformative journey. This section explores practical ways to accomplish this, shaping our children's hearts to be attuned to the love and majesty of our Creator.

The dawn chorus of birds, the vibrant hues of a sunset painting the skies, the laughter of our children; these daily occurrences are gifts that often go unnoticed. Encouraging children to take note of the simple blessings around them is the first step in cultivating gratitude. Challenge them to find three things they're thankful for each day and share them around the dinner table or before bedtime prayers.

In our culture of instant gratification, it's essential to pause and appreciate God's timing, which can often bring unforeseen blessings. When hopes are delayed or desires unmet, use these moments to reinforce patience and trust in God's plans. Share stories of biblical figures who waited faithfully and were rewarded, like Abraham and Sarah, to illustrate the virtue of patience.

Adoration for God flourishes when we are aware of His presence in every aspect of our lives. Create spaces in your home where God's Word is visible—verses of praise on the walls, or a family gratitude journal in the living room, open for anyone to jot down moments of thanksgiving. This physical manifestation of faith serves as a constant reminder to give thanks and praise God.

Modeling a life of gratitude and adoration is perhaps the most powerful tool in a parent's repertoire. Let your children see you in moments of genuine thankfulness. When they observe you praising God amid trials or expressing sincere thanks for everyday blessings, these actions speak volumes. Your life becomes a living lesson in worship.

Faith traditions and holidays offer ripe opportunities to celebrate God's goodness. Whether it's Christmas, Easter, or a personal day where God has acted mightily in your family's life, commemorate these occasions with joy and reverence. Teach them the history and significance of these days to deepen their appreciation and adoration for God's work throughout history.

Music and singing are compelling forms of expressing adoration for God. Integrate worship songs into your daily routine, encouraging children to sing and make a joyful noise unto the Lord. This not only improves their mood but also instills a sense of connection to the divine through melody and praise.

Teach children to pray with a heart of gratitude, not just a list of requests. Guide them in crafting prayers that start with praising God for who He is and what He has done before asking for their needs or desires. This reorientation toward adoration before petition emphasizes God's sovereignty and goodness.

Service to others is a tangible expression of our thankfulness for God's grace. Involve your family in acts of kindness and charity, whether it's volunteering at a local shelter, visiting the sick, or helping a neighbor. As they give, they will learn the joy that comes from a grateful heart that overflows with God's love.

Spend time in nature, observing the masterpiece of creation. Take walks in the park, hike through the woods, or simply sit under the stars. Use these moments to point out the intricacy and artistry of God's handiwork, awakening a sense of wonder and gratitude for the world He has entrusted to our care.

Encourage your children to record their prayers and answered prayers. Keeping a prayer diary can strengthen their faith and deepen their sense of gratitude as they reflect on the faithfulness of God in responding to their needs and the needs of others.

The discipline of fasting, when introduced appropriately, can heighten gratitude for God's provision. Teach them the biblical basis for fasting and how it refocuses our hearts and minds on God, magnifying our appreciation for His sustenance and presence in our lives.

Include thanksgiving in your family's milestones. Whether celebrating birthdays, graduations or personal achievements, lead with a prayer of thanksgiving to God for His blessings and guidance. This marks life's high points with a spirit of gratitude rather than entitlement.

Scripture memorization is not just an educational task; it's a way to saturate our children's minds with God's promises and character. Encourage them to commit to memory verses that speak of giving thanks and praising God, so these truths may come easily to their lips and hearts in times of both joy and adversity.

Lastly, encourage a life of worship by being attentive to the diverse ways children express adoration. Some may find their heart in service, others in song, some in quiet contemplation of Scripture, or in the passionate sharing of God's love with friends. Recognize and nurture these individual expressions of worship, fostering an environment where each child can develop their unique relationship with God.

True gratitude and adoration for God cannot be mandated; it must be cultivated. It grows from consistent, loving practice and sincere modeling. As we guide our children, let us remember that the attitudes of their hearts will be shaped by the atmosphere of faith and thankfulness we create in our homes. Such a heart will not only worship fully but will also radiate the love and grace of God to those around it.

Chapter 9:
Peer Relationships and Social Challenges

As our journey continues, the landscape of parenting broadens to include the valleys and peaks of a child's social world. In Chapter 9, "Peer Relationships and Social Challenges," we'll navigate the intricate paths of friendships and societal pressures. Our children's peers play a pivotal role in shaping their character, experiences, and, ultimately, their faith walk. This chapter will guide you in equipping your children to form meaningful and edifying relationships, grounded in Christ-centered values. We'll explore how they can stand firm in their faith when faced with peer pressure, making wise choices that reflect the strength of their convictions. With a heart attuned to God's wisdom, you'll be empowered to support your children through their social journeys, preparing them for the upcoming teenage years with grace and foresight. This critical stage of life calls for compassionate engagement, strategic mentorship, and fervent prayer, as we aim to raise children who are not only socially adept but also spiritually resilient.

Guiding Children in Choosing Friends Wisely

As we navigate the complex sphere of peer relationships and social challenges, it's crucial for us to offer our children the compass of wisdom to choose their friends thoughtfully. Just as trees are known by their fruit, so too can friendships significantly influence a child's growth and character development. It is, therefore, a pivotal concern for parents committed to nurturing their child's spiritual and moral integrity.

To begin with, it's important to understand that friendship is more than shared interests or casual companionship. It's a deep connection that can either enrich your child's life or lead them astray. Encourage your child to seek out peers whose values reflect those you've nurtured within your family. Teach them that true friends will respect their faith and morals without pressing them to compromise.

Plant the seed of discernment early on by discussing what qualities make a good friend. Love, respect, honesty, and loyalty are not just admirable traits but biblical principles. Open the pages of Proverbs with your child and explore how this book of wisdom speaks of companionship. Let the scripture be a lamp unto their feet in friendships just as it is in life.

Modeling the friend-making process is tantamount. Let your children see you choosing and nurturing friendships that are uplifting and edifying. More is caught than is taught, and by observing how you interact with friends, they will learn to form meaningful relationships themselves.

There will be times, undoubtedly, when children will be faced with the allure of popularity at the expense of principle. The desire to fit in can be incredibly strong, but this is an opportunity to gently guide them back to their foundation. Ask reflective questions that will encourage them to think critically about the impact a friendship has on their beliefs and actions.

It's also valuable for children to understand that friendships will come and go—and that this is a natural part of life. Just as the seasons change, so too can friendships evolve or fade, and that's perfectly acceptable. Encourage your child to treasure the moments and lessons from each friendship, knowing that God has a plan for every encounter in their lives.

Set aside time to discuss the day's events with your children, paying particular attention to their interactions with friends. It's in these daily reflections that you can guide them with questions that probe beneath the surface, prompting them to think about who they are in their friendships and who they are becoming.

Encourage your children to engage in activities and groups that align with your family's values. Whether it's a church youth group, a community service project, or a faith-based club at school, these environments can foster healthy friendships that are supportive of their walk with Christ.

It's equally important to help your child understand the influence they have on their friends. Teach them that they are called to be salt and light (Matthew 5:13-16), helping to preserve and illuminate not only their own paths but also to positively impact their friends and those around them.

When your child shares struggles they're facing with friends, avoid the impulse to fix the situation immediately. Instead, use it as an opportunity to empower them to seek guidance through prayer, trusting in the Lord's wisdom to discern the right course of action. Encourage them to ask for discernment and wisdom as James 1:5 promises.

Although boundaries are an essential part of parenting, remember to balance your guidance with respect for your child's autonomy. Overregulating their friendship choices can backfire, leading to rebellion and secrecy. Instead, be a trusted adviser who they can approach freely without fear of judgement or overreaction.

Don't forget the power of prayer in all of this. Pray for your child's friendships, for the Lord to send godly companions into their life, and for your child to have the strength to be a good friend. Foster a home environment where prayer is the first response and not the last resort.

At times, your child will make friendship choices that concern you. When this happens, it is imperative to approach the situation with grace and understanding. Conversation is key, not criticism. Help them weigh the pros and cons of the friendship and guide them back to scripture.

Finally, remember that the ultimate friend we want our children to be ever drawn to is Jesus Christ. By anchoring their hearts in His love, they will not only seek out His likeness in their friendships but also strive to be that kind of friend to others. In John 15:13, they can learn about the greatest display of friendship—one that lays down life for another.

In journeying alongside your child in their quest for genuine, enriching friendships, you are not only shaping their social circle but sharpening their character. Stand firm in love, lead them with scripture, and let the Holy Spirit guide them through the beautiful maze of relationships. Through these measures, wisdom will be their companion, and virtue their lifelong friend.

Navigating Peer Pressure with Scriptural Wisdom

As parents, one of the heart's most earnest prayers is for our children to stand strong in the face of peer pressure, holding onto their values with grace and courage. Peer pressure is an undeniable force that tests the spiritual fortitude of young souls, guiding them on a path that's not always aligned with the wisdom of the Scriptures. It's our role, as their guardians, to equip our children with the scriptural insights necessary for navigating these social challenges.

Understanding that peer pressure can be both overt and subtle, we must begin by grounding our children in who they are in Christ.

Building their identity on the solid rock of God's Word assures them that they are loved, valued, and created with a divine purpose. This knowledge serves as an anchor, providing them the strength to resist the waves of societal conformities.

Excursions into the Scriptures, like visits to a grand and wise mentor, can reveal stories of individuals who faced and overcame great peer pressure. Daniel, for instance, chose to honor God over the edict of the king and remained steadfast despite the threat of the lions' den. His example can inspire our young ones to hold firm in their convictions, even when the consequences loom large.

Conversations at home should also highlight that every choice has a consequence. Galatians 6:7 reminds us that we reap what we sow. Helping our children foresee the potential outcomes of succumbing to peer pressure fosters foresight and encourages them to make decisions that align with their faith and expected results.

Empower your children by practicing scenarios where they may confront peer pressure. Just as Jesus was tempted in the wilderness, our children, too, will face their own tests. Equip them with scriptural responses, akin to Jesus's stands, as He countered each challenge with the authority of Scripture.

The Book of Proverbs is a treasure trove of wisdom pertinent to resisting peer pressure. Proverbs 1:10, "My son, if sinful men entice you, do not give in to them," serves as a direct warning. Involve your children in studying these Proverbs, discussing the ageless wisdom found within, and applying them to modern-day scenarios.

Moreover, let us remind our children that they are not alone in their struggles. 1 Corinthians 10:13 promises that God will not let them be tempted beyond what they can bear. Assure them that God provides an escape, a way to withstand the urge to follow the crowd.

This fosters a reliance on divine help and steers them away from a sense of isolation.

Encourage your children to build relationships with peers who share their values. Two are better than one, as Ecclesiastes 4:9-10 teaches us, for they can help each other succeed. When your child has friends who also respect and honor Christian principles, they can support each other in resisting negative peer pressure.

Peer pressure often plays upon our deepest insecurities, but 1 Peter 2:9 describes us as a chosen people, royal priesthood, and holy nation. When children understand their royal and holy standing before God, it reshapes their perception of acceptance and success. Peer approval pales in comparison to the honor of being chosen by God.

Equip them, too, with the armor of God spelled out in Ephesians 6:10-18. This passage is not mere metaphoric imagery but a practical blueprint for standing firm in the face of adversity. Teach them to gird their lives with truth, righteousness, peace, faith, and salvation. These are not just spiritual concepts but practical everyday choices that protect against the pressures to conform.

Introduce your children to the concept of servant leadership as taught by Jesus. In peer relationships, it's easy to fall prey to the desire for popularity or to submit to louder voices. But Mark 10:43-45 flips the script on what it means to lead and to influence, positioning service as the true north of leadership and providing a God-honoring pathway through relational dynamics.

Keeping an open and non-judgmental line of communication is key. When your children err, and they might, be ready to listen, forgive, and guide, rather than condemn. Like the father in the parable of the Prodigal Son, be a safe haven where they can find guidance and restoration.

Finally, model the strength to resist peer pressure in your own life. Our children watch us, and when they see their parents choosing integrity over convenience, choosing to love when it's difficult, and standing firm on their beliefs, they learn to do the same. Your walk with God speaks louder than any sermon.

Remember, parenting is a journey of guiding your child's heart over controlling their outward behavior. It's about nurturing a compass that points to God, no matter the social storms they may face. Encourage, guide, and pray for your children, knowing that the One who began a good work in them will carry it on to completion.

In this journey of raising children resilient in the face of peer pressure, may you be bolstered by the understanding that the Scriptures are not just literature from the past but a living guide that speaks into the very challenges your children face. Filled with timeless wisdom, the Word of God is an ever-present helper and the sharpest tool in your parenting arsenal. Lean on it, and find strength in its power.

Preparing for the Teenage Years

As your child's journey through childhood progresses towards the teenage years, their social landscape evolves dramatically. These years can be filled with growth, but they also come with unique challenges, especially concerning peer relationships. As a guiding light in your child's life, you're tasked with preparing them for this influential period, drawing from our Creator's wisdom and the nurturing presence of Jesus. Understanding the significance of forming healthy peer relationships, anchored by Christian values, is crucial during adolescence.

Navigating peer relationships during the teenage years requires discernment both from parents and teenagers. The social pressures that come with these developing connections can sometimes sway our children away from their moral compass. Instill in your child the importance of surrounding themselves with peers who respect and share their faith values. Encourage open conversations about their friendships, providing them with the assurance that you're there to support and not judge them.

Begin by reinforcing the importance of individuality and God-given uniqueness. As your children enter their teen years, they may feel compelled to conform to peer expectations. Remind them that God has created them with a purpose and that their personal values should not be compromised for acceptance. This principle will serve as an anchor as they navigate the tumultuous waters of social acceptance and peer pressure.

Equip your teenager with scriptural knowledge that they can draw upon when faced with challenging situations. The wisdom found in verses like 1 Corinthians 15:33, "Do not be misled: Bad company corrupts good character," provides a clear guideline for choosing friends and understanding the impact those friends can have on their lives.

Also, involve your teenager in youth groups and Christian-based activities where they can meet like-minded peers. Through such fellowship, they can build strong, supportive friendships grounded in mutual respect and shared beliefs. These connections can prove to be lifelines when their faith is challenged.

Enhance your teen's emotional intelligence and communication skills. Teach them to express their feelings and stand firm in their convictions with grace and love. The ability for your teenager to communicate effectively with their peers, saying "no" when necessary, can't be underestimated. This ability is a powerful tool when coupled with a faith that empowers them to make the right choices, even when it's difficult.

Assert the value of integrity and moral courage. Discuss real-life scenarios they may encounter and explore the possible choices they could make. These discussions can build their confidence and provide them with practical strategies for facing peer pressure without feeling isolated.

Practice active listening with your teens, honoring their thoughts and perspectives. This shows them that their voice matters and equips them with the confidence to share their beliefs and boundaries with others. When teens feel heard at home, they're more likely to speak out and influence their peer groups positively.

Maintain a balance between guiding your teen and granting them independence to make their own decisions. While it's natural to want to protect them from potential missteps, remember that each choice they make is an opportunity for growth. Offer trust and allow them the space to use the discernment you've been nurturing.

Embrace the power of prayer together with your teenager. Involve them in praying for their friendships and the social challenges they face. This shared spiritual discipline strengthens their reliance on God and reinforces the understanding that they're never alone in their struggles.

Encourage your teens to serve others, both in and outside the church community. Service projects and mission trips can broaden their perspective, help them build a compassionate worldview, and connect them with peers who also value altruism. This shared sense of purpose can create deep and enduring bonds.

Help your teenager to develop patience and understanding in their relationships. Remind them that, as Christ is patient with us, we should also be with others. This patience and grace will enable them to navigate misunderstandings and conflicts in a constructive manner that can strengthen, rather than damage, relationships.

Address the issue of romantic relationships with sensitivity and openness. Emphasize the Christian perspective on dating and purity, and discuss the importance of choosing a partner whose values align with their own. Provide them with the scriptural support and the assurances they need to face the complex feelings that can accompany these relationships.

Be an example of the loving relationships you wish them to emulate. Your marriage and friendships should reflect the love, respect, and integrity you're teaching. When teenagers witness these qualities in action, they understand what to look for and what to strive for in their own relationships.

Finally, let your children know that no matter what, they can come to you with their struggles. Whether they face rejection, make mistakes, or need guidance, your constant love and the wisdom of the Scripture will provide a safe harbor. Reiterate that through Christ, there is always grace and the chance to start afresh.

In preparing for the teenage years, remember that these formative times offer fertile ground for lessons that will last a lifetime. Peer relationships and social challenges will come and go, but the foundation you set in Christ will endure, guiding your teenager towards a future of fulfilling relationships and a strong, unwavering faith.

Chapter 10:
Health, Wholeness, and Christian Stewardship

As we turn the page to "Health, Wholeness, and Christian Stewardship," we hold a mirror to our daily practices, casting light on the profound interconnection of physical health and spiritual well-being. It is here that we delve deeply into the ethos of bodily temples given by our Creator and the responsibility that comes with such a gift. Imagining, with compassionate nuance, the teachings we instill in our children about their physical existence, we intertwine the fibres of health education with the golden threads of Christian stewardship. Our guidance through this journey must be as gentle as the morning dew yet consistently firm, much like the sturdy branches of an olive tree providing both sustenance and shade. Through this process, we shall pursue balance, allowing the hushed whispers of rest to harmonize with the vibrant echoes of activity and the nourishing rhythm of a well-considered diet, all resonating with the beauty of God's design. This delicate harmony cradles our children's development, shaping their understanding that a healthy lifestyle is not merely a personal crusade but a vital contribution to the tapestry of the community at large, woven with the threads of faith and love.

Teaching Children About Their Bodies from a Christian Perspective

As we traverse the nuances of nurturing young ones in accordance with the Word of God, it becomes imperative to address a facet of life we sometimes approach with trepidation: teaching our children about their bodies. This delicate topic must be broached not only with care and sensitivity but firmly rooted in the Christian perspective that affirms both the wonder and stewardship of the human form as created by our Heavenly Father.

Within the sacred pages of Scripture, we find that our bodies are described as temples of the Holy Spirit, entrusted to us to care for and respect. It's our task as parents and caregivers to instill this profound truth within our children – that their bodies are masterful creations, deserving of honor and care. Emphasizing this reverence can start simply, with toddlers learning to express gratitude for their hands and feet, eyes and ears, each part beautifully wrought by God for a purpose.

Fostering open dialogues about the body should begin early, adapting the depth and complexity of the conversation to the child's developmental stage. For the youngest members of our families, we might start by naming body parts as we give thanks for them during nightly prayers, ensuring they understand that each part, seen and unseen, is part of God's intentional design.

As children grow, the narrative expands. They may question how and why God created them as they are. Here, it's vital we respond with both biological truth and scriptural backing, offering explanations that honor their inquisitive minds while directing them back to God's wisdom and provision. Affirming that 'God knit me together in my mother's womb' personalizes this idea (Psalm 139:13).

Body image concerns often surface as children observe the world around them and compare themselves to others. It's in these moments we encourage looking not to societal standards but to God's view of them, highlighting Scriptures such as Psalm 139:14, which declares them 'fearfully and wonderfully made'. By rooting their self-image in the immutable love and design of God, children can build resilience against fleeting and often unattainable societal benchmarks.

Fostering an understanding of privacy and boundaries is another fundamental aspect. It is crucial for children to know that their bodies are personal and that they have the right to protect their physical space. Teaching them about appropriate and inappropriate touch supports their sense of agency over their bodies and aligns with the belief in honoring God's temple.

As puberty approaches, frank discussions regarding bodily changes must be underscored by the continuous theme of growth as part of God's plan. Delving into the marvels of how bodies are divinely engineered to develop not only prepares them for what lies ahead but also celebrates their journey in becoming the individuals God intends them to be.

Equally important is the conversation about purity and intimacy. Framed within the context of God's design for marriage and relationships, these discussions must encapsulate the value of patience, self-respect, and the sacredness of the union between a husband and wife, all of which should be addressed at an age-appropriate level.

In an age where the culture often dictates confusing messages about gender and sexuality, returning to the bedrock of biblical truth fortifies young hearts and minds. It provides clarity amid the chaos, anchoring them in the belief that their identity is first and foremost found in Christ, and it is He who guides all aspects of their lives, including their understanding of gender and sexuality.

Nurturing healthy habits, from hygiene to exercise, can be anchored in scriptural teachings. For example, encouraging good stewardship of their bodies as a way to honor God can motivate children to care for their physical selves without crossing into vanity or self-obsession.

This journey of bodily understanding is also an opportunity to teach compassion and acceptance. As children become aware of their own bodies, it's a chance to nurture empathy, understanding that others have been crafted with equal care by God, despite any differences in form or function. Feeding the mind with such wisdom fosters a heart that cherishes all of God's creation.

Dealing with injury or illness becomes a moment to reflect on dependence and trust in God. Physical challenges can be instructive in demonstrating the temporary nature of our earthly vessels and the eternal steadfastness of God's love and healing power. Amidst hardships, scripture becomes a source of comfort and strength.

The salient concept of modesty, grounded in a scriptural context, propels us to guide our children in recognizing the importance of presenting themselves in ways that honor God and respect themselves and others. In this conversation, the focus isn't on rules for the sake of rules but on the deeper principles of dignity and self-worth.

Through each of these teachable moments and discussions, prayer and reflection must remain central. By praying with our children for understanding and appreciation of their bodies, we invite the Holy Spirit to guide their hearts and minds, nurturing a relationship with God that encompasses all aspects of being.

In this faithful journey of teaching our children about their bodies from a Christian perspective, we hope to lay a foundation of health, wholeness, and godly stewardship. With diligence and prayer, we steward the next generation to walk in wholeness and holiness, embodying the love and wisdom of Christ in every aspect of their lives.

Balancing Physical Activity, Rest, and Nutrition

Nourishing the body God has entrusted to us involves a delicate equilibrium of movement, tranquility, and sustenance. As you shepherd your family along the path of health, envision each day as a tapestry woven with strands of physical activity, restful repose, and the colors of the earth's bounty. Encourage your children to delight in the joy of play, to dance, run, and skip—not merely for the sake of exercise but as an expression of the grateful heart that beats within them. Instill in them the wisdom to listen to their bodies when they whisper for rest, understanding that even Christ withdrew to silent places to renew His spirit. At your table, let meals become more than just eating; make them a celebration of nourishing the temple of the Holy Spirit, with foods that are as close to how God created them, rich in the nutrients that enable us to thrive. By modeling this harmony, you'll teach your children that caring for the physical self isn't separate from our spiritual lives but is a form of worship, respecting the Creator by honoring His creation.

The Role of Health in Spiritual Well-being

As we guide you through the multi-faceted journey of Christian parenting, we recognize health as a critical component of nurturing not only the body but also the spirit. The interweaving of physical health and spiritual well-being cannot be overemphasized in the context of raising children with robust moral and spiritual foundations. Indeed, our bodies serve as temples of the Holy Spirit (1 Corinthians 6:19-20), and as such, our physical wellness contributes substantially to our ability to connect with and honor God.

Tending to the health of ourselves and our children is to acknowledge and respect the divine craftsmanship of our Creator. In promoting good health practices, we are teaching our young ones stewardhip of their bodies, entrusted to them by God. Instilling in them an understanding that bodily health influences spiritual clarity and fervor prepares them for a life dedicated to His service.

The daily routines we establish for balanced nutrition, regular exercise, and adequate rest not only shape our children's physical development but also their mental and emotional equilibrium. When our bodies thrive, they become vessels capable of weathering both physical and spiritual storms, offering resilience in times of challenge and adversity.

Moreover, consider the discipline required to maintain health—this in itself is a spiritual exercise. By following healthy lifestyles, our children learn about self-control, a fruit of the Spirit (Galatians 5:22-23), which carries over into their spiritual lives. It's a training ground for resisting temptations and making choices aligned with their faith.

Encouraging children to value their health means instilling a sense of responsibility for their well-being, which echoes in their spiritual lives. We teach that just as one wouldn't neglect their health, neither should one neglect their spiritual condition. Both require regular attention and care.

When our children fall ill, it is an opportunity to understand the fragility of life and to develop empathy. Through sickness and recovery, they can experience the healing power of prayer and the comfort of relying on God's strength, fostering a deeper spiritual connection and reliance on the Lord.

Physical activity, for instance, can be a form of praise and worship. Exercise is not only a chance to improve fitness but also moments for reflection, meditation, and appreciation of one's health. Teaching our children to see the wonder in their movement and capabilities draws their minds to the Giver of all good things.

Nutrition plays a role as well. When we select our sustenance with care and gratitude, we honor God's provision. By consuming what nourishes and refraining from what degrades our bodies, children can learn that making healthy choices is a form of respect to God and His creation.

Sleep and rest are no less vital. Teaching our little ones that rest is integral to God's design, evidenced by the Sabbath, is to offer them the wisdom of balance. Kids who understand the rhythm of work and rest are more likely to grow into adults who understand the value of spiritual replenishment and sanctuary.

Health also entails emotional and mental well-being. Nurturing a sound mind within a sound body is critical for children to fully engage in worship and service. A heart unburdened by emotional strife is freer to experience the joy of the Lord and share it with others.

Consider proverbs such as, "A joyful heart is good medicine" (Proverbs 17:22). The Bible informs us of the intrinsic link between joy, health, and spiritual life. In teaching our children to find happiness in their faith, we invite a wholesomeness that fortifies against worldly ills.

Conversely, recognizing when to seek support for mental health issues reaffirms that asking for help is not a sign of weakness, but of courage and wisdom. It is embracing the biblical truth that we are meant to bear each other's burdens (Galatians 6:2). In doing so, we help our children find spiritual community and support that are essential at every stage of life.

As we guide our children in balancing physical activity, rest, and nutrition, we set the stage for a lifetime of valuing their divine design. Moreover, by seeing health as a reflection of spiritual well-being, children can form habits and attitudes that glorify God through their bodies, building a foundation for holistic worship. The health of our families should be a joyful expression of our commitment to the wholeness God desires for us, one that resonates in both their hearts and spirits.

In attending to our children's health, the path we carve out is one that leads them naturally to steward their earthly bodies in preparation for eternal life. As we partake in this sacred responsibility, we nurture not only healthy individuals but also devout followers, who embody the strength and vitality of their convictions.

Last of all, may we, as parents and guardians modeling Christian principles, remember to apply this harmonious approach to our own health. By doing so, we become living testimonies to the blessings of intertwining physical wellness with spiritual vitality, offering the most compelling lesson our children can witness. We thus pave the way for them to not simply tread through life but to soar on wings like eagles, fortified in body, mind, and spirit.

Chapter 11:
Technology, Media, and Christian Ethics

In an age where screens light up our homes more often than candles, parents are tasked with guiding their children through the digital era with thoughtfulness and discernment. As we venture into the complex realm of technology and media, it's vital to uphold the Christian ethics that illuminate our path. Children are impressionable; the information they absorb and the entertainment they indulge in can shape their hearts and minds. Thus, when we set boundaries for screen time, it's not merely about limiting hours, but nurturing souls to seek the good, the true, and the beautiful in a virtual landscape. We're called to carefully discern the media choices that enter our homes, ensuring they honor the values we hold dear—those that echo the love and wisdom of Christ. It's about instilling a natural inclination to turn away from that which dims their light in favor of what kindles their spirit. In the face of the insidious nature of online dangers, our guidance stands as a beacon, protecting innocence while teaching our young ones the art of cautious engagement. As we stand at the intersection of the world's highways and the narrow path, let's choose, together with our children, the route paved with virtue, paving the way for them to use technology, not as an escape, but as a tool for God's glory.

Setting Healthy Boundaries for Screen Time

In today's fast-paced digital world, screen time is an all-but-inevitable part of family life. As we navigate the waters of technology within our homes, it's critical for parents to establish healthy boundaries that reflect our Christian ethics. Just as we meticulously select nourishment for our bodies, so must we carefully curate the media that feeds our minds and spirits.

Firstly, let's acknowledge the need for intentionality when it comes to screen time. The Bible doesn't address digital technology directly, but it does guide us to make wise choices. Philippians 4:8 urges us to focus on whatever is true, noble, right, pure, lovely, and admirable. This scripture can serve as a compass for the types of media we permit in our households and the amount of time we devote to screens.

In setting boundaries, we must assess the purpose behind screen time. Is it for education, entertainment, or perhaps communication? Blades are useful tools in the kitchen, yet we teach our young ones to handle them with care. Similarly, we must guide our children in understanding the purpose of technology, using it as a tool rather than allowing it to become the focal point of their lives.

Let us begin by creating a 'family media plan'. This plan would involve a schedule that balances screen time with other important activities such as family devotions, outdoor play, and creative hobbies. A balanced plan can help children learn to prioritize time and responsibilities in alignment with our Christian values.

As a family, openly discuss the reasons behind screen time limits. When children understand the 'why', they are more likely to adhere to the 'what'. Engage them in creating these boundaries, which might include having screen-free zones in the house such as the dining table and bedrooms, encouraging interpersonal connections and restful sleep.

It's also vital that we model the behavior we wish to instill. If we set parameters around screen use for our children but fail to adhere to them ourselves, our teachings lose credibility. We should demonstrate a balanced media life, perhaps by putting away our devices during family time and openly engaging in non-screen based leisure activities.

Consider the content as much as the quantity of screen time. As parents, we're called to be the gatekeepers of what enters our home. This means pre-viewing programs, setting up content filters, and using tools like parental controls to ensure that what our children watch aligns with our Christian beliefs.

Engage with them during screen time to establish a shared experience and to provide immediate guidance. This practice also offers the opportunity for discussion about the values and messages they're being exposed to through media, fostering critical thinking and discernment.

Implementing a 'technology Sabbath' can be a powerful practice in our homes. By choosing a day to rest from screens, we redirect our attention to God and to each other, creating space for restorative activities and spiritual nourishment.

Remaining vigilant and up-to-date with the ever-changing digital landscape is a task we must embrace. Educate yourself about the latest apps, games, and social media platforms that captivate children's attention. Understanding the digital realm enables us to navigate it with wisdom and discernment.

Encouraging alternative activities to screen time is also beneficial. Foster a love for reading, engage in family community service, or explore God's creation together. Such experiences not only reduce screen time but also enrich the spiritual and moral fabric of our family life.

Though restrictions are necessary, the aim isn't solely to limit but to teach responsible usage. Open dialogue about the impact of technology on their spiritual and moral development helps children make wise choices even when parents aren't present.

Recognize that every child is unique, and flexibility in enforcing screen time boundaries is needed. Some children may require more stringent guidelines, while others may thrive with slightly more freedom. Praying for wisdom and discernment is crucial as we customize our approach for each child.

In times of resistance or struggles with these boundaries, it's important to remain patient and compassionate. Gentle reminders of why we choose to limit screen time can reinforce the importance of these values. Challenges in implementing these boundaries can become teachable moments and opportunities for growth.

Finally, celebrate the successes and positive choices your children make regarding screen time. Positive reinforcement cultivates an atmosphere of encouragement, motivating them to continue making sound decisions in alignment with their faith.

By imparting the importance of setting healthy boundaries for screen time and upholding these principles through the lens of our Christian values, we can guide our children towards a balanced life. A life where screens serve their purpose without dominating, distractions are managed with wisdom, and time is spent cultivating a rich, God-honoring existence.

Discerning Media Choices that Honor Christian Values

As we navigate a world rife with technological advances, it becomes increasingly paramount for families to discern what media aligns with their Christian values. Every show, advertisement, or social media post our children encounter leaves an imprint, shaping their perceptions and potentially influencing their behavior. In this crucible of visual and audible stimuli, how can we as parents ensure that their media experience nurtures their growing faith?

The answer lies in becoming meticulous curators of the content that flows into our homes. This means not only monitoring but also actively seeking media that reinforces the principles of love, integrity, and compassion foundational to Christian teaching. It's not just about avoiding the explicit and the untoward but also investing in what edifies and encourages a Christian way of living.

Firstly, consider the powerful role of storytelling. Stories shape our understanding of the world; they teach us about virtue and vice, courage and cowardice. Select films, TV shows, and books that tell stories of heroism, sacrifice, and truth—those that resonate with the Gospel's message. Such narratives inspire our children to emulate these values in their own lives.

Music, too, can be a profound influence. It's not merely a backdrop but a language that speaks to the soul. Embrace songs and hymns that uplift and focus the heart on God's presence and love. Be wary, however, of tunes that, while catchy, may convey messages counter to what we are teaching at home and at church.

It's also essential to support Christian content creators by actively seeking out their work. When you choose books, movies, or music produced by those who share our faith, you are not only filling your family's life with wholesome content but also nurturing a Christian artistic community.

Further, teaching children to be critical consumers of media is imperative. Encourage conversations about what they watch and listen to. Ask them what they liked about a particular story or character, and discuss how it either aligns with or deviates from our faith. Help them to understand that every media choice has the potential to shape character and worldview.

Nonetheless, choices in media should never lead to legalism or fear. We ought not to retreat into a bubble, avoiding all contact with contemporary culture. Jesus engaged with people where they were, using parables relevant to their lives. We too can find balance, knowing when to embrace and when to turn away, always with discernment and grace.

In the digital age, where media is ever-present, setting boundaries is crucial. Discuss as a family what those limits look like, and make decisions together about what is permissible. These guidelines should reflect your family's values and a commitment to prioritizing time spent in fellowship, in God's word, and in service over screen time.

Moreover, be vigilant about the subtleties in media. Sometimes, harmful messages aren't overt but are woven into the fabric of the narrative or the assumptions of a program. Maintain an open dialogue with your children about recognizing these undercurrents and understanding the importance of a worldview anchored in Christ.

Take advantage of Christian media reviews and recommendations from trusted sources. These can be invaluable tools in helping discern choices that are suitable and edifying. These critiques often dive deeper than mainstream reviews and consider the content through a lens of faith.

Moreover, do not overlook the impact of news and current events. Balance awareness of the world with the need to shield young hearts and minds from the distress and complexity of some topics. Find age-appropriate ways to discuss current affairs, grounding your conversations in prayer and scriptural truths.

Remember, too, that children will imitate what they see modeled. If we want our children to make discerning media choices, we must also practice this discernment. Let your own media habits provide a blueprint for your children, demonstrating a life that is not dictated by screens but enriched by meaningful connections and experiences.

As we integrate media into our lives, prioritize activities that involve interaction over isolation. Engage with media as a family, whether that's co-viewing a movie, discussing a book, or playing an edifying game together. Use these opportunities to connect and reflect on the values portrayed.

Finally, pray for guidance in making media choices. The Holy Spirit is our counsellor, able to steer us through the vast sea of options. Include your children in these prayers, teaching them to seek divine wisdom as they encounter the ever-changing media landscape.

In conclusion, our task is not easy, but it is holy work. By making media choices that honor Christian values, we lay a foundation that will support our children's spiritual growth, imbue them with strength to resist the contrary pressures of the world, and inspire them to live out their faith with confidence and joy.

Parents, guardians, as stewards of our children's hearts and minds, let's commit to being intentional with every click, every play, and every page turn. Let's harness media as a tool for good, transforming potential pitfalls into opportunities for affirmation and grace. Together, with wisdom and prayerful consideration, our families can thrive, grounded in Christian values and illuminated by the light of Christ in all we consume and create.

Protecting Children from Online Dangers

The world of technology, with its plethora of platforms and devices, has fashioned a new frontier for parenting. In an era where the digital realm can seem as vast and treacherous as the open seas, it's critical to navigate these waters with the same vigilance as one would in guarding their child from physical harm. As Christian parents, instilling values such as wisdom, discernment, and purity in our children is a formidable task, especially when faced with the complex challenges of the online world.

Navigating cyberspace requires a balance. Too often, the internet is seen as a void where danger lurks behind every click, yet it's also a place replete with vast resources for learning and growing. Our children need guidance to discern the good from the harmful. Just as we teach them to look both ways before crossing the street, we must teach them to pause and evaluate the virtual roads they travel.

First and foremost, familiarize yourself with the digital terrain. The same way you'd learn about your child's school and friends, take time to understand the apps, games, and social media platforms they're using. This knowledge isn't about invading privacy but equipping yourself to have informed conversations about safe online practices.

Open dialogue is the bedrock of trust and understanding. Start conversations early about the importance of privacy and the potential risks of sharing personal information. Encourage your children to come to you with anything online that makes them feel uncomfortable, uncertain, or threatened. It's essential that they view you as a sanctuary of wisdom and peace, rather than a figure of judgment or punishment.

Set clear boundaries and expectations for online behavior, anchored in Christian ethics. This might include rules about not engaging with strangers online, being kind and respectful in all digital interactions, and avoiding content that doesn't align with our faith's values. With these guidelines, you create a moral compass that can guide them even when you're not present.

Filtering and monitoring are practical tools and not a sign of distrust. A multitude of software options can help shield your children from inappropriate content. However, filters are not a substitute for parental involvement. They are merely a layer of protection in a multi-faceted approach to online safety.

Be proactive in educating your children about the concept of digital footprints. Every comment, photo, or profile update is a permanent addition to their online legacy. Instill a sense of responsibility about the lasting nature of online actions, much as we sow seeds that grow into fruit bearing trees. Teach them to only post content they would be proud of, content that reflects the light of Christ.

Social media can be a battleground for self-esteem and identity, challenging even adults. Guide your children in understanding their intrinsic worth as children of God, not to be dictated by likes, shares, or follows. Ensure they build their esteem on the rock-solid foundation of God's love, not the shifting sands of social opinion.

With the prevalence of cyberbullying, prepare your children to be both resilient and compassionate. Equip them with the armor of God so that they might withstand harsh words and also be empathetic supporters to others experiencing these trials. Encourage them to foster a culture of kindness both offline and on, echoing the teachings of Christ.

Developing a sense of mindfulness and presence can also serve as a buffer against the relentless pace of digital life. Encourage times of digital detox, where the family unplugs and reconnects with each other and with God. These moments create spaces for reflection and appreciation of life without the interruption of notifications and news feeds.

The anonymity of the internet can sometimes lead to temptations and moral hazards. Discuss with your children how the principles that guide us in the physical world should not be abandoned online. Encourage them to practice integrity, to act in ways that honor God, even when they believe no one is watching.

Online games and communities can provide a false sense of accomplishment and belonging. It's our role to help our children find meaning and purpose not in virtual achievements but in serving God and others. Help them recognize the fulfillment that comes from real-life experiences and relationships over any digital reward.

Technology can also be a tool for spiritual growth. Direct them to Christian content online, such as devotionals, worship songs, and sermons that can nourish their faith. This shapes their understanding that the internet can be a conduit for good, a place to grow closer to God and understand His Word in unique ways.

Be their role model in all things, including your digital conduct. If we spend our free moments with eyes fixed to screens, we broadcast a message regarding our values. Instead, let them see you reading Scripture, praying, or engaging in activities that reflect your faith. Actions will always speak louder than words.

Lastly, entrust your efforts and your children to God through prayer. Our Father, who sees all, knows the challenges we face and is always available for guidance and support. Pray for protection over your children in every realm—in the physical and in the digital. Lean on Him to fill in the gaps that our human limitations create.

We may not be able to shield our children from every online risk, but we can certainly pave a path through the digital landscape that is informed, intentional, and imprinted with the footsteps of Christ. As we foster these principles within our home, we also contribute to a broader culture of online safety and respect.

Chapter 12:
The Art of Christian Leadership and Influence

In the midst of a world often entangled in egocentrism, parenting offers a stage to exhibit the quintessence of Christian leadership—a symphony of humility and service. Imagine guiding your child not by mere instructions, but by infusing the delicate balance of authority with gentleness, exemplifying the tender might of Jesus' own leadership. The art of Christian leadership in the home is not about power, but the empowerment of our young ones to discern and embrace ethical values. It is the quiet, persistent work of nurturing those entrusted to our care to walk with integrity, to make choices steeped in wisdom and love, thereby equipping them to hold the torch of faith in future roles within society. Through fostering leadership skills that bloom from the fertile soil of selflessness and servant-hood, your guidance as a parent cradles the next generation in truth and propels them towards their God-given destiny.

Fostering Leadership Skills Rooted in Humility and Service

As we've journeyed through the intricacies of Christian parenting, the importance of a strong moral foundation has emerged time and again. Now, we delve into an attribute often overlooked in our hurried society: humility. True leadership, the kind that's rooted in Christian values, isn't about puffing oneself up but about kneeling down to serve others. It's a paradox of strength; for in our service, we lead, and in our humility, we achieve greatness.

Modeling leadership begins in the nuanced dance of everyday life. Show your children that even the smallest act of kindness is a cornerstone of leadership. When you hold the door for a stranger, share a word of encouragement, or help someone in need, you're embodying the leadership of Christ. It's through these gestures that children learn leadership isn't about titles or accolades; it's a matter of the heart.

Within our homes, we can encourage children to take on small responsibilities that nurture a servant's heart. Delegate tasks not just as chores, but as their contribution to the family – their act of service. In doing so, they learn that each role, each effort, contributes to the wellbeing of the whole. It's not merely a dish washed or a floor swept; it's a practice in stewardship and responsibility.

It's essential to balance service with humility, emphasizing that neither is blind obedience or self-deprecation. Instead, humility is recognizing that every person has value, and every task has purpose. When your child achieves something, celebrate their effort and talent, but also help them to see the contributions of others in their success. Encourage them to share credit and remain grounded.

As your children grow, involve them in greater acts of service. Volunteering as a family can be a powerful experience, immersing your children in environments where they see the tangible impact of their actions. Whether it's serving at a soup kitchen, participating in a community clean-up, or visiting the elderly, these experiences are ground zero for servant leadership.

Dialogue with your children about the leaders throughout history who have exemplified servant leadership. Point out figures like Mother Teresa and Martin Luther King Jr., who leveraged their leadership for the betterment of others. Challenge your children to see how these individuals used their influence not to gain power but to empower others.

Leadership requires decision-making, and children will be faced with countless choices. Guide them on how to make decisions that align with Christian values. Teach them to weigh options with prayer, consult Scriptures, and seek wise counsel. Equip them with the confidence to choose paths that may not be popular but are principled, showing them that true leaders walk in integrity, even when alone.

Remember that humility is sometimes learned through failure. When children stumble or face setbacks, it's a chance to show them how leaders behave in the face of adversity. Encourage resilience, reflecting on what can be gained from the experience. Help them understand that every leader has moments of defeat, but what defines them is their response.

As they encounter success, we have an opportunity to teach our children about the dangers of pride. Instill in them the importance of giving thanks to God for their abilities and achievements. Help them to remain humble by turning their eyes towards service and gratitude rather than self-glory.

At times, humility means standing up for what is right, even if it means standing alone. Inspire your children to be defenders of the marginalized and to speak up for justice. Use biblical examples of individuals who showed incredible courage and humility, such as Esther and Daniel. Reveal to them that leadership often requires a quiet strength to uphold truth and kindness.

Don't shy away from difficult discussions about leadership and power. Teach your children that being a leader doesn't mean dominating others, but rather lifting them up. Speak about the gentleness of Christ and his assertiveness when it came to matters of injustice.

Encourage your children to nurture their talents and gifts with a spirit of humility. Help them to see that their abilities are blessings meant to serve others, not just themselves. This perspective ensures that as their skills grow, so does their inclination to use them for the greater good.

Commit to ongoing conversations about the leaders your children admire. Discuss what qualities make those individuals excellent models of Christ-like leadership. Instill in them that leadership is not inherent, but developed through conscious choice and action.

Lastly, pray regularly with your children for discernment and wisdom in their journey towards leadership. Let them hear your own prayers for guidance and humility in your role as a parent and leader within your family. Your example will speak volumes and provide the spiritual support they need to grow.

By fostering leadership skills rooted in humility and service, we set a path for our children to become influencers who mirror the love and grace of Christ. It is in these moments of teaching, serving, and nurturing that we witness the unfolding of their potential as future leaders who prioritize the welfare of others above their own. This journey is a testament to the enduring impact of Christian values in shaping a world that reflects God's kingdom on earth.

Encouraging Ethical Decision-Making

As we cultivate leadership within our family, a cornerstone of our efforts must be the nurturing of ethical decision-making. True leadership cannot flourish without a strong moral compass. We are tasked with the profound responsibility of guiding our young ones toward paths that not only align with our Christian faith but also uphold the ideals of integrity and righteousness.

Begin with the understanding that our children watch us, absorbing our actions and reactions. In this silent observation, they learn about right and wrong. Emphasize transparent honesty in your interactions, not only with your children but with everyone around you. Your life is the most influential sermon they will ever witness.

Encourage questioning and exploration within a safe environment. Children should feel comfortable to ask about ethical dilemmas and moral uncertainties. When they do, respond with patience and reference Scripture whenever possible to nurture a biblically grounded rationale for morality.

Conversations about character and values should be routine, not just saved for Sunday lessons. Proactively discuss scenarios your children might face, such as bullying, cheating, or lying, and explore together how Christ's teachings inform our responses to these challenges.

Empower your children to make decisions. Start with small, daily choices and as they grow, help them understand the consequences of their decisions. Always relate these back to the broader impact on their character, their relationship with God, and their influence on others.

Share stories of ethical role models from the Bible, such as Daniel, Esther, or Joseph, who faced moral trials and prevailed through their unwavering faith. Highlight contemporary examples, too, of individuals who embody Christian ethics in the face of adversity.

In the complex tapestry of today's society, teach context and discernment. It isn't simply about choosing right over wrong, but understanding the subtleties and nuances of situations. Guide them to pray for wisdom, as James 1:5 advises, so that they will not be double-minded but assured in their actions.

Confront mistakes openly when they happen. Use these as teachable moments to discuss repentance, forgiveness, and the grace of God. It's crucial for children to grasp that while sin has its consequences, God's love remains steadfast.

Encourage them to seek counsel from trusted Christian mentors, be they youth leaders, pastors, or wise family members. These figures can provide different perspectives and share their own experiences with ethical decision-making.

Instill in your children a powerful sense of stewardship. Just as we are temporary caretakers of Earth, so too are we trustees of the truth. They should seek to protect and foster honesty and integrity, be it in school, among friends, or in the community.

Talk about the value of delayed gratification and self-control, virtues that are vital in resisting temptation and choosing long-term gain over short-term pleasure. Explain how scripture lauds these traits and how they fortify ethical decisions.

Maintain a culture of accountability within the family. Set expectations and consistency in upholding rules and moral standards. When children understand that everyone, including parents, is accountable, they learn the importance of responsibility in their personal and social lives.

Praise and reinforce ethical decisions, no matter how small. Affirmation can cement a commitment to ethical behavior and motivate your children to continue making moral choices.

Model the humility to accept feedback and admit your own ethical mistakes. Showing your children that growth and learning are lifelong processes encourages them to always strive for moral improvement and integrity.

Finally, wrap all these efforts in prayer. Regularly pray with and for your children, asking God to fill their hearts with discernment, courage, and an unwavering commitment to walk in His footsteps, no matter the challenge. In doing so, you craft a foundation for ethical decision-making that can withstand the pressures of the world and echo throughout eternity.

Preparing Young Christians for Future Roles in Society

As we steer the course of nurturing the next generation, we acknowledge the vast expanse of society's landscape that our children will navigate. In a world ever-changing, the constant that remains is the call for Christians to be salt and light. As caregivers, our mission is to prepare our young ones not merely to find their place in society but to shape it with the wisdom, compassion, and moral fortitude grounded in Christian values. This undertaking, both noble and daunting, is enriched by tailoring our guidance to the individual strengths and calling of each child under our care.

The premise of Christian leadership is unlike any worldly counterpart. It is servant leadership that Jesus Christ himself modeled - one that does not seek personal gain but rather the wellbeing of others (Philippians 2:3). Instilling this in our youth begins in the small, often unnoticed moments of family life. It buds in the genuine compliments we give our children for acts of kindness, in the encouragement when they stand for what is right, and the fortitude they observe in us during times of trial.

Ponder for a moment the parable of the talents (Matthew 25:14–30). We see in this imagery powerful lessons on responsibility, initiative, and the consequences of inaction. Thus, we are compelled to guide our young charges in discovering their God-given talents, nurturing those gifts, and inviting them to be proactive stewards of those abilities. Whether their strengths lie in intellectual acumen, emotional intelligence, artistic expression, or any other area, we must fuel their passion for utilizing these talents in service and leadership.

In a society where the pursuit of power and status is prevalent, we must present a different narrative for our children. Leadership is often perceived as wielding control, but let us teach our young that true influence is serving others (Mark 9:35). This teaching is not to be abstract but exemplified in daily life, as we serve alongside our children in community projects, church activities, or simply in how we manage conflict and prioritize the needs of others in our homes.

Another cornerstone of preparing young Christians for society is inculcating ethical decision-making. Ethics grounded in Christian truth should be the compass that guides all choices. Yet, this compass is only as effective as one's familiarity with it. Regular engagement with scripture, discussions about moral dilemmas, and thoughtful reflection on current events in light of biblical principles all serve to fine-tune this moral compass.

Communication cannot be overstated when it comes to imparting wisdom and guidance. How we converse about life's complexities, issues of justice, and matters of the heart will shape our children's perceptions and attitudes. To speak the truth in love (Ephesians 4:15), to listen with a desire to understand, and to engage in dialogue that reflects God's love and justice are skills that will serve our young well as they grow into roles where their words will carry weight and influence.

Bringing the conversation into the public sphere, it is vital to encourage our children to be conversant and confident in discussing their faith. Being ready to give an answer for the hope we have (1 Peter 3:15) means our children need not only knowledge of their beliefs but also the skill to articulate these beliefs respectfully and persuasively. Role-playing conversations, public speaking within safe environments, and teaching logical reasoning are all part of this important development.

Let's never discount the significance of mentorship. In the tapestry of biblical narratives, we observe mentor and mentee relationships that fostered growth and prepared young leaders like Timothy, Joshua, and David. Encourage interactions with godly role models in the community – those who exemplify Christian leadership. Let your children learn from their victories and even their failures, understanding that all experiences can cultivate wisdom for their future roles in society.

We must also seek to create opportunities for leadership. Allow children to take charge of projects, whether it's a charity event, a church program, or even a family activity, to give them a sense of responsibility and ownership. Such experiences are fertile ground for the seeds of leadership to germinate, showcasing the tangible impact of their efforts and decisions on a smaller scale before they face larger societal challenges.

The virtue of resilience is a gift unto society. As parents, it is our duty to teach our children to endure in the face of frustration, to persevere through setbacks, and to remain steadfast when their values are opposed. This resilience is crafted through our reactions to their struggles, the stories of faith we share, and the encouragement we offer when they face their own Goliaths.

A young Christian's desire for societal influence should align with their personal calling. Each one is a unique part of the body of Christ (1 Corinthians 12:12-27), so let us encourage them to seek God's purpose for their lives through prayer and self-discovery. In discovering their vocation, they find a channel for their leadership and influence that is both fulfilling and in service to God's greater plan.

It is crucial to discuss the reality that societal roles sometimes come with opposition and challenges. Equip our youth with the armor of God (Ephesians 6:10-18) so they can stand firm in their faith and values. Teach them the power of discernment, the courage to say "no", and the wisdom to choose battles worthy of their effort and sacrifice.

As they grow, let us encourage our future leaders to foster connections beyond their immediate Christian circles. By understanding and appreciating diverse perspectives, they can become effective ambassadors for Christ who build bridges rather than barriers in all spheres of society.

In conclusion, preparing young Christians for societal roles is an ongoing process. It requires intentionality, adaptability, and a heavy dose of grace. Encourage children to practice leadership and influence daily, remind them of their unwavering value in Christ amidst society's shifting standards, and praise their efforts to shine His light. Through this, we equip them not just to survive but thrive and lead in a multifaceted society anchored by their faith. In doing so, we forge a future where Christian values continue to be a vital thread in the fabric of society, promoting a life of service, integrity, and genuine love.

As we tend to this generational garden, let us have eyes to see the potential within each child and the heart to nurture it. They are the emerging architects of society, the future voices in the choir of discourse, the hands that will build upon our foundation. With divine guidance, our mentorship will empower them to assume their roles with confidence, humility, and an unwavering commitment to the Christian tenets of love and service. May the fruits of our labor be evident in their lives as they influence the world for Christ, one action, one conversation, one relationship at a time.

Chapter 13:
Sowing Seeds for a Godly Legacy

As we reach the closing pages of our journey together, let's reflect on the magnitude of our task and the profundity of our mission. To sow seeds for a godly legacy is no small undertaking. It is the very essence of Christian parenting, the tapestry we weave that will outlast our own lives. This legacy is a beacon of love, faith, and hope that will illuminate the paths of our children long after we have gone.

Throughout this book, we have explored a multitude of ways in which we can anchor our children in Christ's love, from establishing a faith-based home environment to fostering servant hearts. Each strategy and insight, drawn from the wisdom of the gospel, is a thread in the quilt of legacy we offer our children. Remember that every act of love, every word of guidance, is a seed planted in fertile soil.

Our efforts to communicate with compassion and clarity set the tone for a life filled with grace and understanding. When we listen actively and respond with kindness, we teach our children to do the same. It's through these moments of heart-to-heart connection that we build a resilient family, capable of withstanding the ebbs and flows of life.

We've seen how integrating the church community can support our family's spiritual journey. The church is not just a building; it is the body of Christ, walking with us, holding us accountable, and providing a network of support. Leverage this divine collective to fortify your children's faith and your own.

Education is a cornerstone of any legacy. Merging Christian values with learning empowers our children to navigate an increasingly complex world, equipped with the armor of God. Be intentional in the educational paths you choose, ensuring that they are suffused with the light of biblical truths.

In a world that often seems overwhelmingly focused on instant gratification, the commitment to purposeful discipline is an act of love that will shape your children's futures. Discipline woven with love and intention fosters respect, understanding, and self-control in young minds and hearts.

Cultivating a life of worship and praise is a daily renewal of our commitment to the Lord. This practice lays a spiritual foundation in our homes that will resonate through every corridor of your children's lives. Through arts, music, or silent contemplation, worship is our soul's expression of gratitude to the Creator.

The friends and social circles our children choose can significantly influence their development. Guiding them through this process, arming them with scripture, and offering them a safe space to discuss their choices helps them navigate these complex dynamics. Their ability to choose wisely will be a testament to your guidance.

Stewardship of our physical selves is indeed a mirror of our spiritual health. When we teach our children to honor their bodies as temples of the Holy Spirit, we instill in them the value of self-care as a reflection of godly respect. This approach to health, wholeness, and stewardship will serve them throughout their lives.

In an era where technology reigns, setting boundaries and upholding Christian ethical standards is vital. By teaching discernment and protecting our children from online harms, we are equipping them with the tools they will need to walk in faith amidst a digital landscape.

Our children are the next generation of Christian leaders. By nurturing leadership qualities rooted in service and humility, we are paving the way for them to make ethical decisions and exert a positive influence on society. Through our guidance, they learn to lead not with pride, but with a servant's heart.

Each word we've shared, each lesson we've pondered together, has been in service to this noble cause. The culmination of your daily commitment is the emergence of a legacy that stands firm in the Lord, a legacy that blesses your children and your children's children.

It's my fervent hope that the seeds you sow in faith and in line with the strategies outlined here will yield a harvest beyond measure. Be patient, for a legacy isn't typically revealed in the daily grind but in the splendid tapestry revealed over time. Trust in the steady hand of God to guide your planting and to bring forth the vibrant colors of a life richly lived in Him.

May your journey in Christian parenting be blessed with abundant growth, deep connections, and everlasting joy. May the love you share with your children today flourish into a legacy of faith that will resonate through generations. And in this sacred undertaking, may you find strength in the promise that the Lord is with you always, guiding, loving, and nurturing the seeds you sow in His name.

As we close this book and continue the never-ending story of our families, let's embrace the fullest potential of our roles, cultivating, nurturing, and relishing the garden we tend with such care. The legacy we yearn to sow—one of unwavering faith and boundless love—begins with our commitment to living out the truths we so dearly believe. May all glory be to God, as we trust in His faithfulness to bring to fruition the godly legacy we strive so earnestly to establish.

Appendix A:
Resources for Christian Parents

As we've traversed the many dimensions of Christian parenting, we've gathered wisdom and applied faith-based principles in our homes. Yet, there is immense value in expanding our horizons, seeking continuous growth, and delving into resources tailored to support you on this sacred journey of upbringing your children in God's love. Within this appendix, you'll find a collection of materials that serve as a wellspring of inspiration and practical guidance.

Recommended Reading List

Dive into the depths of Christian literature that resonates with your family's journey. These books are beacons of light, offering insights into the heart of parenting with intentionality and a Christ-centered approach:

- *Shepherding a Child's Heart* by Tedd Tripp: A transformative look at the heart of parenting.

- *The 5 Love Languages of Children* by Gary Chapman and Ross Campbell: Helping you speak your child's love language fluently.

- *Parenting with Grace* by Gregory Popcak: A Catholic guide to raising (almost) perfect kids.

- *Boundaries with Kids* by Henry Cloud and John Townsend: A guide to understanding and instilling healthy boundaries.

Family Devotionals and Bible Study Guides

These tools can foster a dynamic and nurturing spiritual atmosphere in your home, enriching your family devotions and deepening your collective journey in faith:

- *The One Year Devotions for Preschoolers*: Daily readings that bring biblical stories to life for young minds.

- *The Family Bible Devotional* by Sarah M. Wells: Stories from Scripture to help you and your kids engage in meaningful discussion.

- *Our 24 Family Ways* by Clay Clarkson: A family devotional guide that fortifies Christian values in everyday life.

Online Resources for Christian Parenting

In our digital era, an abundance of online resources is available at your fingertips. Here are several trusted sources that can offer support, community, and enlightening content:

- Focus on the Family: A global Christian ministry with a treasure trove of articles, broadcasts, and tools for families.

- Christian Parenting: A website that equips parents to navigate the challenges of raising kids with a strong foundation in Christ.

- The Bible App for Kids: Interactive story adventures that help children learn and understand Bible stories in a fun and engaging way.

May these resources serve as compasses to guide you, light that illuminates your path, and encouragement that lifts your spirit. Your role as a Christian parent is pivotal, not just within the walls of your home, but as a beacon that shines into the world, reflecting God's profound love through the nurturing of His young disciples. Hold fast to your mission, fortified by these supports, as you lead your family toward a legacy of faith that endures.

Recommended Reading List

The words we feed our minds and hearts can profoundly shape the paths we walk. As parents aiming to forge a family life steeped in Christian principles, one of the greatest tools at our disposal is a library of insightful, faith-affirming literature. Let's delve into an array of books that promise to invigorate your parenting journey and deepen the spiritual roots of your family.

Firstly, "Shepherding a Child's Heart" by Tedd Tripp offers an outstanding foundation for parents. This book emphasizes the importance of shaping a child's heart rather than just correcting behavior, aligning discipline with the truths of Scripture.

"Parenting with Love and Logic" by Foster Cline and Jim Fay, while not exclusively Christian, provides parents with the practical skills to raise self-confident, motivated children ready to face the world. Its principles harmonize well with Christian teachings of love and stewardship.

For those navigating the intricacies of communication within the family, "The Five Love Languages of Children" by Gary Chapman and Ross Campbell guides parents in understanding the unique ways their children express and receive love, paving the way for stronger, more nurturing relationships.

In addressing spiritual formation, consider "Raising a Modern-Day Knight" by Robert Lewis. This book lays out a framework for fathers eager to lead their sons into authentic, biblical manhood through time-honored rites of passage.

"Bringing Up Girls" and its counterpart "Bringing Up Boys", both by James Dobson, share wisdom on the distinct challenges faced in raising children of different genders. These reads offer a blend of research, psychology, and theology to inform a balanced approach to Christian parenting.

"Boundaries with Kids" by Henry Cloud and John Townsend equips parents with the tools to set appropriate boundaries with their children, crucial for healthy emotional and spiritual development. Learning to say no is framed within the wider context of godly love and guidance.

"Sticky Faith" by Kara Powell and Chap Clark tackles the vital topic of instilling a lasting faith in kids, providing evidence-based practices that help keep children close to Christ and the church as they grow into young adults.

For parents desiring to explore education through the Christian lens, "Educating the WholeHearted Child" by Clay and Sally Clarkson presents a compelling vision for home education that integrates academic learning with spiritual growth and creative expression.

"Raising Kingdom Kids" by Tony Evans challenges and encourages parents to raise their children with a kingdom perspective, reminding them that godly parenting extends beyond the home and into a life of service and witness to others.

Kevin Leman's "Making Children Mind without Losing Yours" injects humor into the serious business of parenting. This book aligns well with Christian values of grace, truth, and love, offering strategies for parents to guide children towards God-honoring behavior without resorting to anger.

As challenges arise, "The Power of a Praying Parent" by Stormie Omartian is a treasure trove of prayers for every aspect of a child's life. This book assures parents of the power of their prayers to protect, guide, and hold their children in God's love.

For deeper biblical insight, "The Jesus Storybook Bible" by Sally Lloyd-Jones brings the stories of Scripture to life in a way that is engaging for both children and parents, illustrating how every story points to Jesus.

In the realm of nurturing a servant's heart, "Raising World Changers in a Changing World" by Kristen Welch inspires parents to instill a sense of mission and generosity in their children, promoting a lifestyle that values giving over getting.

And lastly, "Don't Make Me Count to Three" by Ginger Hubbard provides an empathetic guide to disciplining with wisdom and patience, drawing directly from Scripture to address the heart issues behind children's behavior.

This curated collection of books opens doors to a wealth of wisdom, strategy, and encouragement for parents. As you explore these resources, may each page turn be a step towards a stronger, more faith-filled family. Embrace these tools, pour over their words, and see your family thrive under the nurture of their guidance. This is your invitation into a community of parents committed to raising up the next generation with hearts for Christ.

Family Devotionals and Bible Study Guides

In the journey of nurturing a faith-filled home, family devotionals and Bible study guides stand as robust pillars supporting the fortress of Christian values. These tools are not just books or schedules; they're vessels for spiritual discovery and togetherness, enriching your family's bond with God and with one another.

Creating a routine that includes family devotionals can be both a balm for the soul and an anchor for the day. As you select a devotional, look for one that resonates with your family's interests and spiritual maturity. It might include stories, reflections, and questions that foster dialogue, allowing each family member to explore and express their faith.

Bible study guides, often structured with themes or specific passages for focus, can provide an interactive map for journeying through Scripture. Whether you're delving into the lessons of the Proverbs or wandering the paths of the patriarchs in Genesis, these guides can offer historical context and practical applications to anchor God's Word in your daily life.

Consider age-appropriate materials for your children. For the youngest, brightly illustrated Bible stories that highlight the triumphs and trials of biblical heroes can ignite their imagination. For teens, guides that challenge them to connect biblical principles with real-life situations can be particularly empowering.

However, devotionals and Bible study should be more than reading and discussion. They're about creating moments to experience faith as a living, breathing reality. Engage your children in acting out stories, singing, or even drawing scenes from the day's passage. These activities help to cement biblical truths in young hearts.

One potent approach is to let children take turns leading the devotional. This act nurtures leadership and confidence in their understanding of faith. It's incredible how much insight we can gain from a child's perspective on Scripture.

True transformation starts with consistent practice. Carve time out of your busy schedule to sit down together, free from distractions, and open your hearts to the messages within these guides. Let this be the time when phones are silenced, and the hustle of the day pauses.

Remember, there's no one-size-fits-all devotional. Some families may thrive on daily short reflections, while others may prefer a longer, in-depth study weekly. Start with what feels manageable and meaningful for your family's rhythm.

Incorporate prayer into your study time, intentionally praying over the insights you've gained or lifting up family members as they share their reflections. This not only reinforces what has been learned but also models the power of bringing every aspect of life before God in prayer.

Don't become discouraged if some days, the study doesn't go as planned. There will be times of disinterest or distraction, but persistence is key. A family that returns to God's Word, even after a chaotic day, is building spiritual resilience and a foundation of faith that can withstand the world's distractions.

Be receptive to the Holy Spirit's guidance as you contemplate the Scriptures. Sometimes, a passage or a story may take on a different, more profound meaning in light of current family circumstances, offering comfort or calling for change. Embrace these moments as divine whispers tailored for your family's journey.

Lastly, go beyond the pages of your guides and devotionals. Apply the lessons learned by living them out. Whether it's showing kindness to a neighbor or standing for justice, let the Scriptures come alive in your actions as a family. After all, the most profound lesson for children is watching the biblical truths being lived out by their parents.

As you close each devotional session, take a moment to cherish the spiritual growth occurring within your family. With each story shared and verse uncovered, roots grow deeper, bonds strengthen, and hearts align more closely with the heart of God.

As this chapter unfolds, you'll find that devotionals and study guides are not just supplementary materials in your Christian parenting arsenal; they are essential companions, nurturing the soil from which the life-long journey of faith grows and flourishes within the home you're striving to build.

Online Resources for Christian Parenting

Embarking on the journey of Christian parenting, the digital world at our fingertips offers a treasure trove of resources designed to support and enrich the faith-based family life. As parents seeking to instill Christian values in our children, tapping into these online resources can be incredibly empowering, providing us with guidance, fellowship, and creative ideas for nurturing spirituality at home.

One of the first places to explore is the wide array of Christian parenting blogs. These personal online journals are penned by fellow parents who document their experiences and share their strategies for overcoming the daily challenges of Christian parenting. From tackling tough conversations about faith to sharing scripture-based bedtime routines, these blogs can be a source of both inspiration and practical advice.

Podcasts, with their convenience and variety, offer another rich layer of support. Many Christian leaders and parenting experts host series that tackle subjects ranging from discipline to deepening family faith. While commuting, exercising, or during quiet moments, these audible gems can provide parents with insights and encouragement that resonate with their own parenting journeys.

Interactive forums and social media groups form the backbone of the virtual Christian parenting community. Within these digital spaces, you can engage with like-minded parents from around the world, exchange ideas, request prayers, and offer support to others. The shared wisdom found here is invaluable, as it comes from a pool of diverse experiences and perspectives.

Webinars and online workshops, often organized by churches or Christian parenting experts, bring learning to the comfort of your home. These events cover a range of topics and can range from one-off sessions to multi-week courses, providing deep dives into subjects such as biblical parenting techniques, balancing grace and discipline, or managing family dynamics within a Christian framework.

When it comes to scripture engagement for kids, the internet abounds with resources tailored to making the Bible accessible and engaging for children of all ages. Websites offer animated Bible stories, games, and activities that make learning about God's word both fun and memorable, ensuring that the truths of the scripture resonate with young hearts and minds.

Online bookstores dedicated to Christian literature allow you to browse through a vast selection of parenting books, devotionals, and children's Bibles, making it easy to find the right resources for your family's spiritual growth. Many such stores provide detailed reviews and recommendations to help you make informed choices.

Music streaming services and websites can be a wonderful avenue for discovering Christian music that brings worship into the home. Whether looking for songs to sing along with your children or instrumental hymns for peaceful evenings, these platforms can become a vital part of creating an atmosphere of praise in your household.

Software and mobile apps designed to help families pray together and reflect on daily devotions can also play a key role in establishing a routine of spiritual mindfulness. Whether it's a prayer reminder app or a family devotionals app, technology can assist in integrating prayer into your family's everyday life.

With the increasing concern about screen time and internet safety, there are several Christian organizations that offer guidelines and tips on managing technology within the family. These resources help parents navigate the digital terrain, ensuring that their children's online experiences remain positive and within a framework that honors Christian ethics.

Educational websites provide a wealth of Christian-based learning materials, including lesson plans, worksheets, and printable activities that are excellent for homeschooling families or for supplementing public or private education with Christian teachings.

Fundraising and outreach platforms give families the opportunity to engage in service projects and missions from their own homes. Participating in these activities can help children understand the importance of giving and serving, fostering a servant's heart that aligns with Christ's teachings.

For parents of teens and pre-teens, there are specialized online resources that offer guidance on navigating the unique challenges of these developmental stages from a Christian perspective. These include discussions on dating, dealing with peer pressure, and preparing youth for leadership roles in a complex world.

Mental health resources from a Christian viewpoint are increasingly available online, addressing the intersection of faith and well-being. These resources often provide advice, counseling options, and support networks vital for parents dealing with family members experiencing emotional or mental health issues.

Finally, don't overlook the value of online sermons and church services. Many churches stream their services and offer sermon archives on their websites, allowing families to join in worship even when they can't be there physically. This resource can help ensure that your family remains connected to a church community, a fundamental aspect of Christian parenting.

As we continue to navigate the pathways of raising children in a Christian home, let these online resources serve as our companions, guiding lights, and sources of endless wisdom. Thank them for their presence, utilize them with discernment, and above all, let the love of Christ be the cornerstone of all we do in our parenting endeavors.

Online Review Request for This Book

If this guide has ignited in you a deeper passion for weaving Christian values into the tapestry of your family's life, lighting your path as you guide your children to grow in faith, love, and wisdom, please consider sharing your journey and insights by leaving a review online. Your experience could serve as a beacon of hope and inspiration to countless other parents striving to cultivate a home where faith flourishes and love abounds.

Printed in Great Britain
by Amazon

47633406R00081